Two-Hour
Silk Ribbon Embroidery

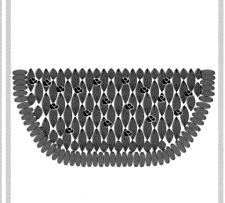

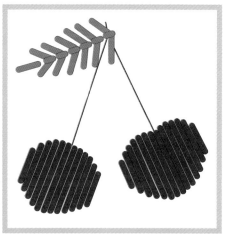

I LOVE YOU

Two-Hour
Silk Ribbon Embroidery
Over 200 Designs

Malissa Williams

Sterling Publishing Co., Inc. New York
A Sterling/Chapelle Book

For Chapelle Limited

Owner: Jo Packham

Editor: Leslie Ridenour

Staff: Malissa Boatwright, Kass Burchett, Rebecca Christensen, Marilyn Goff, Amber Hansen, Shirley Heslop, Holly Hollingsworth, Susan Jorgensen, Susan Laws, Barbara Milburn, Pat Pearson, Karmen Quinney, Cindy Rooks, Cindy Stoeckl, and Nancy Whitley

Photographer: Kevin Dilley for Hazen Photography

Designers: Joy Anckner, Jodi Crompton, Kathy Hackford, Monica Morby, Gaila Shupe, and Sharon Trease

Library of Congress Cataloging-in-Publication Data Available

Williams, Malissa.
    Two-hour silk ribbon embroidery : over 200 designs / Malissa Williams.
        p.   cm.
    "A Sterling/Chapelle book."
    Includes index.
    ISBN 0-8069-8613-1
    1. Silk ribbon embroidery.   I. Title.
TT778.S64W55   1996
746'.0476—dc20

96-9926
CIP

10 9 8 7 6 5 4 3 2 1

A Sterling/Chapelle Book

First paperback edition published in 1999 by
Sterling Publishing Company, Inc.
387 Park Avenue South, New York, N.Y. 10016
© 1996 by Chapelle Limited
Distributed in Canada by Sterling Publishing
% Canadian Manda Group, One Atlantic Avenue, Suite 105
Toronto, Ontario, Canada M6K 3E7
Distributed in Great Britain and Europe by Cassell PLC
Wellington House, 125 Strand, London WC2R 0BB, England
Distributed in Australia by Capricorn Link (Australia) Pty Ltd.
P.O. Box 6651, Baulkham Hills, Business Centre, NSW 2153, Australia
Printed and bound in Hong Kong
All rights reserved

Sterling ISBN 0-8069-8613-1 Trade
               0-8069-8715-4 Paper

Every effort has been made to ensure that all of the information in this book is accurate. However, due to differing conditions, tools, and individual skills, the publisher cannot be responsible for any injuries, losses, and/or other damages which may result from the use of the information in this book.

If you have any questions or comments or would like information about any specialty products featured in this book, please contact:

Chapelle Ltd., Inc.
P.O. Box 9252
Ogden, UT 84409

Phone: (801) 621-2777
FAX: (801) 621-2788

Introduction

Welcome to the time-honored and ever popular tradition of silk ribbon embroidery.

In choosing pieces to share with you, we selected traditional floral motifs, whimsical designs and dimensional projects to appeal to a wide audience.

Designers eagerly contributed their artistic abilities, their fabulous creative ideas, and, of course, their beautiful stitching.

The result of this combined talent is a wonderful collection of more than 200 ribbon embroidery designs.

We have included step-by-step instructions for many common embroidery stitches, appliqué techniques, dimensional ribbon work, and painting on fabric.

Additional designs which provide optional color combinations and variations of motifs are also included with several of the embroidery pieces.

Enjoy!

—Malissa Williams

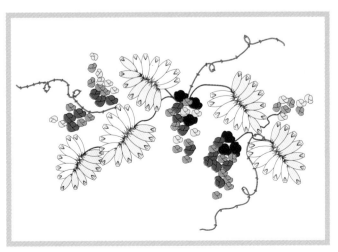

Contents

Contents

Silk Ribbon Embroidery General Instructions

This section is your guide to silk ribbon embroidery. Step-by-step instructions follow for many common embroidery stitches, appliqué techniques, dimensional ribbon work, and painting on fabric.

Silk Ribbon

The key to any successful ribbon embroidery project is the ribbon that you use. You can use either pure silk ribbon or synthetic ribbon if you wish. There are advantages and disadvantages to each. You will find that silk ribbon behaves differently than synthetic ribbon.

Pure silk ribbon is the strongest natural fiber for its weight. It dyes beautifully and is tougher than cotton. It is also resilient, meaning it will never flatten but will always spring back into shape. However, you must take care when exposing some colors of silk ribbon to moisture as they tend to bleed. Synthetic ribbon, on the other hand, is more color fast and easier to care for. It is also very strong and resilient. Both fibers reflect light, revealing luster and beauty that typify ribbon embroidery.

To complete each project you will need to purchase the colors that are outlined.

Cut the ribbon into 18" lengths to reduce the chance of the ribbon fraying while stitching. Because of the delicate nature of silk ribbon, it can easily become worn, losing some of its body. If this happens, moisten the silk ribbon and it will self-restore. There may be slight color hue differences between strands.

Where more than one ribbon is listed per stitch in the outline, combine the ribbons when threading the needle.

Fabric

All designs can be stitched on a fabric of your choice. It is recommended that you stretch your fabric taut on a hoop before you begin stitching the design. Also, all appliqué work should be completed before stitching with silk or synthetic ribbon. Instructions for appliqué begin on page 16.

Floss

DMC floss colors may be required for each project. When listed, this 6-strand embroidery floss should be separated into one or more strands according to the project instructions.

Needles

The barrel of the needle must create a hole large enough for the silk ribbon to pass through. The ribbon will hide the hole made by the needle. If the ribbon does not pull through the fabric easily, a larger needle is needed. Also, the eye of the needle must be large enough for the ribbon to lay flat when threaded. Choose a needle pack that includes chenille needles in sizes 18 to 22. Use a regular embroidery needle when stitching with DMC embroidery floss.

Tip: Rather than threading and unthreading the same needle, keep several needles on hand threaded with the different colors of silk ribbon used for each project.

Silk Ribbon Embroidery Techniques

Threading and Locking Silk Ribbon

Pull about 3" of silk ribbon through the eye of the needle. Pierce the 3" portion of silk ribbon about ½" from the end. Pull back on the opposite end until it locks securely around the eye of the needle; see Diagram 1.

Diagram 1

Knotting the End of Silk Ribbon

To create a Soft Knot prior to stitching, drape the silk ribbon in a circular manner to position the end of the silk ribbon perpendicular to the tip of the needle. Pierce the end of the silk ribbon with the needle, sliding the needle through the silk ribbon as if to make a short basting stitch. Pull the needle and silk ribbon through the stitched portion to form a knot at the ribbon end; see Diagram 2.

Diagram 2

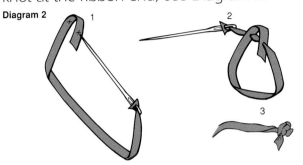

Manipulating Silk Ribbon

One of the most important aspects of silk ribbon embroidery is manipulation of the silk ribbon. For most stitches the silk ribbon must be kept flat, smooth, and loose. You must use your thumb and the needle to manipulate the ribbon as you stitch or the silk ribbon may curl and fold, affecting the appearance of your design; see Diagram 3.

Diagram 3

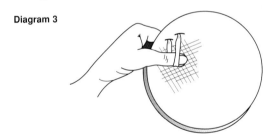

Follow the numerical order of stitches according to the outline for each project. Untwist the silk ribbon during each stitch and use the needle to lift and straighten the ribbon. Pull the silk ribbon gently to allow the stitches to lie softly on top of the fabric. Exact stitch placement is not critical, but you will want to make certain any placement marks are covered by silk ribbon stitches. You may add a few extra petals or leaves by using any leftover ribbon. There are no mistakes, only variations. Be creative with your stitching!

To End Stitching

Secure your stitches in place for each flower

or small area before beginning a new area. Do not drag the ribbon from one area to another. Tie a slip knot on the wrong side of your needlework to secure the stitch in place and end ribbon.

Transferring Patterns Using Dressmaker's Carbon

All project diagrams in this book are actual size unless otherwise noted. Enlarge diagrams if indicated and transfer to fabric following the steps outlined below:

- When stitching on new garments or washable fabric, remove sizing and wrinkles by first washing, drying, and ironing.

- Purchase a package of dressmaker's carbon at your local notions store. Using project diagrams, follow manufacturer's instructions to transfer the design from book pages to fabric. For transferring on black fabric, transfer the design first to a white piece of paper and then trace with a dressmaker's pen.

Caring for Your Projects

It is recommended that you spot clean only as some colors of silk may bleed. Clothing that needs to be cleaned, may be hand-washed with mild dishwashing detergent. If needed, carefully press around embroidered design.

Silk Ribbon Embroidery Stitches

Note: The stitch is shown using either ribbon or floss, but it applies to stitching with either.

Backstitch

Come up at 1 and go down at 2, to the right of 1. Come up at 3, to the left of 1. Repeat 2-3, inserting the needle in the same hole that was 1.

Bead Stringing

Bring the needle to the front of the fabric. Thread on the desired number of beads. Without tying off the thread, reverse the needle; take it back down through the original hole in the fabric and tie off on back.

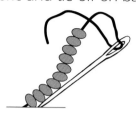

Beading Stitch

Using one strand of floss, come up through fabric. Slide the bead or button onto the needle.

For a bead, push the needle back down through fabric. Knot off each bead.

For a button, take needle down through second hole and through fabric. Knot off.

Bow—Tacking

Tie a bow with the silk ribbon. Thread a needle with embroidery floss. Using floss, come up under the silk ribbon, which is lying flat on fabric. Tack the ribbon in place, leaving streamers loose.

Bullion Stitch

Bring needle up at 1 and down and 2. Needle must come back up at 3, which is where it originated. Do not pull needle through. Wind floss around needle six or seven times. Hold the coil and needle firmly with thumb and forefinger and pull needle and ribbon through. Turn coil back and insert needle back into fabric at 4. To make bullion curve more, wind more floss.

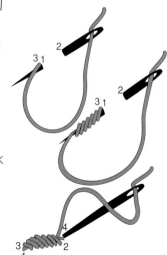

Bullion Lazy Daisy Stitch

The Bullion Lazy Daisy Stitch is completed as Lazy Daisy, but tacked with a bullion stitch.

Bring the needle up at 1. Keep the ribbon flat, untwisted and full. Put the needle down through fabric at 2 and up through at 3, but do not pull through.

Loosely wrap ribbon around needle tip one to three times, as indicated in stitch guide. Holding finger over wrapped ribbon, pull needle through ribbon for a completed Bullion Lazy Daisy.

Cascading Stitch

The Cascading Stitch can be done starting with a bow or just using ribbon to "cascade" streamers through design.

If starting with a bow, tie bow, leaving streamers long enough to work cascade through design. Thread streamer on needle, stitch down through fabric where bow placement is desired, and come back up at start of cascade effect. This will hold the bow in place.

Come up at 1 and go down at 2. Come back up at 3, allowing ribbon to twist and lie loosely on the fabric. Go down again at 2 and come up at 3, making a small backstitch. This keeps the cascading in place.

Chain Stitch

Bring needle up at 1. Keep the ribbon flat, untwisted and full. Put the needle down through fabric at 2 and back up through at 3, keeping the floss under the needle to form a loop. Pull the floss through, leaving the loop loose and full.

To form the next chain loop, which holds the

previous one in place, go down at 4 and back up at 5. Continue to form each chain loop in the same manner. Finish with a short Straight Stitch over the bottom of the last loop to secure in place.

Colonial Knot

Come up at 1. Drape the ribbon in a backward "C". Place the needle through the "C".

Wrap the ribbon over the needle and under the tip of the needle forming a figure 8. Holding the knot firmly on needle, insert the needle through the fabric close to 1. Hold the ribbon securely until knot is formed on top of fabric.

Coral Stitch

This stitch is worked horizontally from right to left.

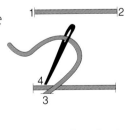

Come up at 1. Drape the ribbon across the fabric to the left and hold. At the appropriate interval, go down through fabric to the top of the ribbon at 2 and come back up at 3, below the ribbon. Bring the draped ribbon under the tip of the needle. Pull the needle and ribbon completely through to form a knot. Continue in the same manner, creating the Straight Stitch with the knot for a completed Coral Stitch.

Couched Stitch

Complete a Straight Stitch the desired length of the design. Make certain ribbon is flat.

Make short tight Straight Stitches across base to "couch" the Straight Stitch (1-2). Come up on one side of the ribbon at 3. Go down on the opposite side of the ribbon at 4. Tack at varying intervals.

Decorative Lazy Daisy Stitch

Bring the needle up at 1. Keep the ribbon flat, untwisted and full. Put the needle down through fabric at 2 and up through at 3, keeping the ribbon under the needle to form a loop. Pull the ribbon through, leaving the loop loose and full. To hold the loop in place, go down on other side of ribbon near 3, forming a Straight Stitch over loop for a completed Lazy Daisy.

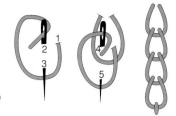

With the same or another ribbon color, come up at 4 and go down just inside the top of the loop, forming a Straight Stitch inside Lazy Daisy Stitch for a completed Decorative Lazy Daisy.

Fly Stitch

Bring the needle up at 1. Keep the ribbon flat, untwisted and full. Put the needle down through the fabric at 2 and up at 3, keeping the ribbon under the needle forming a "U".

Pull the ribbon through, leaving the ribbon drape loose and full. To hold the ribbon in place, go down on other side of ribbon at 4, forming a Straight Stitch over loop. The length of the Straight Stitch may vary according to the desired effect for a completed Fly Stitch.

Folded Rose

Thread and knot a small needle with floss to match ribbon and set aside.

Using an 8" piece of ribbon, finger-press a 45–degree fold to create an L-shape (A). Fold and press the horizontal leg to the back so it extends to the left (B). Fold the vertical leg to the back so it extends downward (C). Fold the

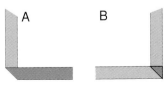

horizontal leg to the back so it extends to the right (D), and repeat.

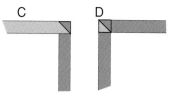

On reaching the ends of the ribbon, hold the last fold and its leg firmly between thumb and forefinger, letting the folded section release itself (E). Pull the other leg gently through the folds. Using the threaded needle, tack base of rose at center and tack in place (F).

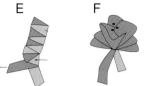

Free-Form Flower

Use a 2" piece of ribbon. Fold each end under about ⅛". Baste along one long edge of the ribbon with one strand of sewing thread or floss. Gently gather ribbon to create a petal the desired length. Knot to secure ruffled effect. Stitch ribbon in place along the gathered edge.

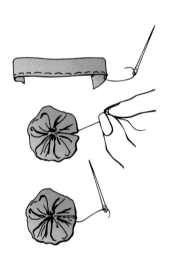

French Knot

Come up at 1; loosely wrap once around needle. Place needle at 2, next to 1. Pull taut as you push needle down through fabric. Carry across back of work between knots.

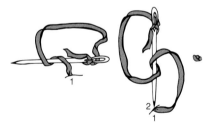

Loop Stitch

Come up through fabric at 1, form a small loop and go down at 2, piercing ribbon.

Lazy Daisy Stitch

Bring the needle up at 1. Keep the ribbon flat, untwisted and full. Put the needle down through fabric at 2 and up through at 3, keeping the ribbon under the needle to form a loop. Pull the ribbon through, leaving the loop loose and full. To hold the loop in place, go down on the other side of the ribbon near 3, forming a Straight Stitch over loop.

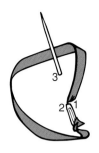

Leaf Stitch

For tip of leaf, make a small Straight Stitch. Make slanted Fly Stitches by coming up at 1, going down at 2 and up at 3. Straight-stitch over ribbon. Continue to fill leaf. Complete Leaf with a Straight Stitch.

Long & Short Stitch

Work the foundation row, alternating long and short Satin Stitches, following the contours of the shape to be filled. Keep stitches close together so that fabric is not visible. On the next row, fit stitches of equal length into spaces left by short stitches in previous row. Continue until shape is filled.

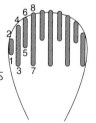
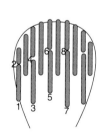

Loose Running Stitch

Follow instructions for Running Stitch (see page 14), making stitches full and loose.

Loose Straight Stitch

Follow instructions for Straight Stitch (see page 15), making stitches full and loose.

One-Twist Ribbon Stitch

Follow instructions for Ribbon Stitch (see page 14), adding a twist in the ribbon before pushing the needle back down.

Open Lazy Daisy Stitch

Bring the needle up at 1. Put the needle down through fabric at 2 and up through at 3, keeping the ribbon under the needle to form a loop. Pull the ribbon through, leaving

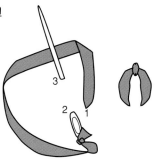

the loop loose and full. To hold the loop in place, go down on other side of ribbon near 3, forming a Straight Stitch over loop.

Outline Stitch

Bring the needle up at the end of the line at 1. Keep the ribbon to the right and above the needle. Push needle down at 2 and back up at 3.

Padded Straight Bud Stitch

This stitch is made up of a Padded Straight Stitch and two Straight Stitches with a single common point.

Begin with a completed Padded Straight Stitch.

Then come up at 1. Go down at 2, keeping the ribbon flat and completing a Straight Stitch. Repeat 1–2 on opposite side of center stitch.

Padded Straight Stitch

Form a Straight Stitch slightly shorter than desired finished length. Then come up at 1 and go down at 2 to cover. Keep the ribbon flat, loose and puffy for a completed Padded Straight Stitch.

Pinecone Stitch

Come up at 1. Extend ribbon its full length and twirl needle so that the ribbon coils, but not so tight that it buckles (A).

Gently hold the ribbon at the mid-point and insert the needle back into the fabric a short distance from 1 (B).

Pull the needle through until only the eye sticks up through the fabric. Release the ribbon and it will automatically twist back on itself (C).

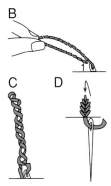

Gently smooth the entire length of the twisted ribbon and pull the needle through to the underside. The ribbon will bunch up as you pull the ribbon through the fabric. Allow the bunched ribbon to remain on the surface of the fabric. Lay the bunched ribbon over on its side and shape as a pinecone. Tack the tip of each pinecone in place with a needle and embroidery floss (D).

Pistil Stitch

This stitch creates the look of a Straight Stitch with a

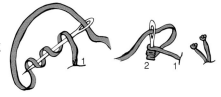

French Knot on the end. Bring needle up through fabric at 1; smoothly wrap thread once (twice for a larger knot on end) around needle.

Hold thread securely off to one side and push needle down through fabric at 2, the length of the Straight Stitch portion of the stitch. Pull taut as you push needle through fabric.

Plume Stitch

Bring needle up through fabric at 1; push the needle down at 2, approximately ⅛" in front of 1. Form a loop, making sure to keep the ribbon flat and smooth.

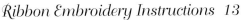

Securely hold the loop and come back up at 3, through the ribbon at the base of the loop. Form another loop by going down at 4, approximately ⅛" in front of previous loop base.

To secure the last loop, come up through the ribbon at the base of the last loop and make a Straight Stitch.

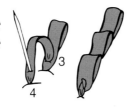

Ribbon Stitch

Come up through the fabric at the starting point of stitch. Lay the ribbon flat on the fabric. At the end of the stitch, pierce the ribbon with the needle. Slowly pull the length of the ribbon through to the back, allowing the ends of the ribbon to curl. If the ribbon is pulled too tight, the effect of the stitch can be lost. Vary the petals and leaves by adjusting the length, the tension of the ribbon before piercing, the position of piercing, and how loosely or tightly the ribbon is pulled down through itself.

Running Stitch

Work a line of Straight Stitches with an unstitched area between each stitch. Come up at 1 and go down at 2.

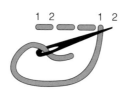

Satin Stitch

This stitch may be worked vertically, horizontally, or diagonally. Stitches may be the same length or in graduations. Keeping ribbon smooth and flat, come up at 1 and go down at 2, forming a Straight Stitch. Then come up at 3 and go down again at 4, forming another smooth Straight Stitch that is touching the first. Repeat to fill design area.

Spider Web Rose

Using two strands of floss, securely work Straight Stitches to form five spokes (A). These are anchor stitches to create the rose with ribbon.

Bring the ribbon up through the center of the spokes (B). Weave the ribbon over one spoke and under the next spoke, continuing around in one direction (clockwise or counter-clockwise), until the spokes are covered (C, D and E). When weaving, keep ribbon loose and allow to twist.

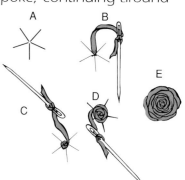

Split Stitch

Come up at 1, and go down at 2. Split the stitch in the middle, as the needle comes out at 3, and go down at 4. Repeat to fill area.

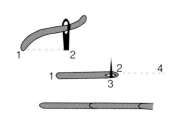

Stem Rose

From left to right, make the first short stitch at the center of the rose. Come up at 1, and insert needle down through fabric at 2. Bring needle up at 3 (halfway between 1 and 2). Moving in a counterclockwise direction, continue circling around the center, lengthening outer stitches until rose is completed. Take needle to back of fabric to finish.

Stem Stitch

Bring the needle up at the end of the line at 1. Keep the ribbon to the right and below the needle. Push needle down at 2 and back up at 3.

Straight Stitch

This stitch may be taut or loose, depending on desired effect. Come up at 1 and go down at 2 at desired length.

Tacked Ribbon

Using one needle threaded with embroidery floss, come up under the silk ribbon, which is lying flat on the fabric.

Tack the ribbon in place. Come up again at desired interval and tack (A). To turn the ribbon flow in another direction, tack the ribbon with the floss from underneath (B) and fold the ribbon over the floss (C).

Tacking

Using one strand of floss, take very small Straight Stitches to secure ribbons to each other or to fabric.

Threading

Weave ribbon or floss in and out of an already established stitch as in Woven Running Stitch.

Twisted Straight Stitch

Follow instructions for Straight Stitch (see above), adding a twist before taking the needle down through fabric.

Whipped Running Stitch

Complete the Running Stitches first.

To whip the Running Stitch, go under the first stitch from 1 to 2. (Be careful not to pierce the fabric or catch the Running Stitch.) Come up on the other side of the stitch. Keeping ribbon flat, wrap over the stitch and go under the next Running Stitch at 3, and then at 4. Continue in the same manner.

Whipped Straight Stitch

Make a Straight Stitch coming up at 1 and down at 2. Come back up at 1; wrap the ribbon around the Straight Stitch, bringing it over the top of the stitch and sliding the needle under the Straight Stitch. (Be careful not to catch the fabric or stitch when wrapping.) Repeat twice.

Go down at 3, under the whip stitch. This will cause the whip stitch to curve for a completed Whipped Straight Stitch.

Whipping

Weave ribbon or floss over and under an already established stitch as in Whipped Running Stitch.

Woven Ribbon Stitch

Bring ribbon up through fabric, and make vertical Satin Stitches to fill shape (A).

Begin horizontal Satin Stitches at top left of shape. Come up through fabric and weave ribbon over and under each vertical stitch (B).

Upon reaching end of row, drop down one ribbon width and weave back across vertical stitches, alternating weave. Continue until shape is completely filled (C).

Woven Running Stitch

Complete the Running Stitches first.

To weave the Running Stitch, go under the first stitch from 1 to 2. (Be careful not to pierce the fabric or catch the Running Stitch.) Continue under the next Running Stitch at 3, returning to other side of line. Continue in the same manner.

Ribbon Embroidery Instructions   15

Appliqué General Instructions

Appliqué

Appliqué is the art of applying fabric cutouts or other materials to a background to create a decorative pattern. The following terms are often used in appliqué work.

Background: Material to which motifs are appliquéd.

Basting: Stitches used to hold motifs in place on the background until secured by some means.

Dimensional Ribbon Appliqué: Tacking pre-made ribbon-work flowers and other pre-made ribbon designs to a background.

Fused Appliqué (Bonded Appliqué): Use of fusible fabric adhesive or iron-on interfacing to bond the design to the background.

Hand-Stitched Appliqué: Hand-stitching fabric cutouts to a background.

Template: A reference drawing of the desired finished appliqué. It is also used as a tool to make patterns.

> The fused method of appliqué—fusing the motifs to a background—is used for projects in this book.

Tools

Note: The tools used are dependent on the means of transferring the design and the method of appliqué used for the project.

Basting thread
Cardboard
Cotton thread or similar synthetic thread in standard and quilting length
Craft knife
Double-sided fusible web
Dressmaker's carbon or chalk
Dressmaker's grid paper
Dressmaker's ruler
Fabric glue
Fabric markers
Florist's wire
Frame or embroidery hoop
Iron, ironing board, pressing cloth
Iron-on interfacing
Light table
Needles: beading, chenille, embroidery, small quilting, and hand sewing; size should be appropriate for fabric
Paints and colored pencils
Pencils: hard and soft, depending on use
Photocopy machine
Pins
Ruler
Scissors: embroidery, fabric, fine-point, paper, pinking sheers
Sewing machine with embroidery function
Tape measure
Thimble
Tracing paper

Fabrics & Threads

All kinds of fabrics can be used for appliqué–plain, patterned, smooth, textured, thick, and thin. The type and style of fabric used depend on the desired look of the finished product and the skill of the crafter. Cotton fabrics are the most popular in appliqué, and are among the easiest to use. Unwoven fabrics, like felt and leathers, are particularly easy to cut and handle and can be used by both beginner and expert alike. Other specialty fabrics, like silks and satins, require skill and care but add sophistication to a piece.

It is best to use like background fabric with like motif fabric, because they will react and behave the same way.

It is also important to take into account the scale of any patterns printed on fabric. Small motifs can be very versatile and will "read" even in a small piece. Larger motifs have a limited number of uses and cannot be seen if the cutout is small.

Also keep in mind how easily a fabric frays. A fabric that frays very easily may be hard to work with, and the edges will have to be secured in some way.

Preparing Fabrics

All fabrics should be clean and pressed (if possible) before using. Make certain the fabric is preshrunk and colorfast if the finished piece will be washed. Also, make certain the grain line is straight by pulling out a weft thread near the edge of the fabric and cutting along the gap.

Positioning the Design

Most designs may be positioned by eye, but some need more precision. To find the center of the design, fold the paper pattern into quarters and mark two pencil lines along the folds. To check if the exact center has been located, draw a diagonal from corner to corner. If it intersects the middle of the crossed horizontal and vertical lines, you have found the exact center of the design.

The center of the fabric can be found in a similar manner. Fold the fabric in quarters and mark the lines with basting stitches. When transferring the design to the fabric, use the pencil and basting lines to check the alignment.

Transferring the Design

Template: The first step in transferring the design is to make a full-scale outline drawing of the design on tracing paper (template). Enlarge the design as needed, using a photocopier, or by hand, using dressmaker's grid paper. Number each separate part of the design in a logical order of assembly, starting with the background and moving to the foreground. Use this full-scale template to mark the background, to make patterns for the motifs, and as a reference during the construction of the piece.

Window or Light Table: The simplest means of marking the design on the background is tracing, using a light table or a bright window. Of course, this method only works if the background is lightweight and/or light colored.

Dressmaker's Carbon: Another means of marking the design on the background is to use dressmaker's carbon paper. Do not use office carbon paper as it will leave indelible marks. Since dressmaker's carbon comes in many colors, choose a carbon paper that is closest in color and tone to the background fabric but that can still be seen. Be certain to follow the manufacturer's directions.

Patterns and Chalk: Another way to transfer the design is to make cardboard or paper patterns and use dressmaker's chalk, fabric markers or a soft pencil to mark the design. This method is not quite as accurate as the first two and it is harder to mark the placement of motifs if they are not a part of the outer edge of the design.

Tracing Paper: Tracing paper can also be used to mark the outline. Pin the tracing paper to the background fabric, then pin or baste along the lines. Tear the paper away. This method is not as accurate as tracing the design directly onto the fabric or using dressmaker's carbon.

Note: It is easier to transfer the design to the back of a fabric if the fabric has a pile. Make certain that you transfer a mirror image of the design.

Making Patterns

Plan the construction of the piece carefully. Sometimes it is easier to overlap pieces than to fit them together exactly.

The tracing or the dressmaker's carbon methods can be used to transfer the design onto the motif fabrics as well as the background. If neither method is feasible, patterns must be made for the motifs to ensure they are cut precisely. The pattern can be made from a variety of materials. X-ray film, stencil plastic, or thick tracing paper are all good choices because they are semitransparent.

Trace each piece of the design from the full-scale template onto tracing paper. Copy the design numbers and mark the grain lines on each piece of the design. Cut out each pattern piece. The pattern can then be transferred to a thicker material if desired.

Cutting Out Motifs

Cut on a flat surface so the fabric does not pucker or draw. Be certain to add seam allowances if necessary. If using a paper pattern, pin the pattern to the fabric and cut out as with any other pattern. If using a thicker pattern, place the pattern on the fabric, pin in place, and mark the design with dressmaker's chalk, fabric markers, or a soft pencil.

Assembling Appliqué

When the design has been transferred to the background by tracing or with dressmaker's carbon, simply place the motifs over the marked outlines. If another means has been used, the motifs can be positioned by eye, using the full-scale template for positioning. Another way of placing the motifs is making a tracing of the design on transparent material and placing it on top of the background. Then, slide the motifs between the two and pin or baste in place.

Keeping Fabric Flat

When doing hand appliqué, good basting is essential. A motif should be basted in place with stitches running both directions. Always start from the center at point 1 to prevent any puckering of the fabric. Then baste outward to 2. Baste again from point 1 to 3, and so on. Additional basting may be required.

An embroidery hoop can be used to hold fabric taut. If the area to be appliquéd is too large for an embroidery hoop, a frame can be used to pull fabric flat.

Fused Appliqué

1. Note: This method is most often used as a preparation for sewing rather than an independent method. Use this method without securing stitches only for infrequently used items. Trace reverse design on nonadhesive (paper) side of double-sided fusible web (outline will be a mirror image of motif). Cut out web motif, allowing a small margin.

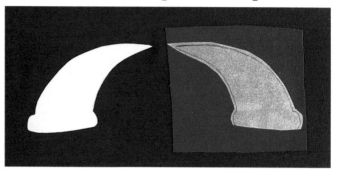

2. Iron unbacked (adhesive) side to appliqué fabric, matching grain lines and following manufacturer's instructions. Cut out motif with sharp embroidery scissors.

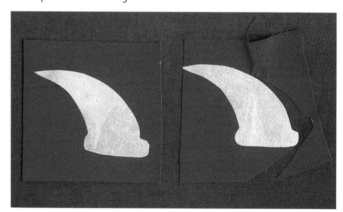

3. Mark placement of motif on background. Peel away backing paper, and iron motif to background, following manufacturer's instructions. Repeat Steps 1–3 for all appliqué pieces. Begin working ribbon embroidery.

Dimensional Ribbon Appliqué Instructions

Dimensional Ribbon Appliqué

Note: For designs using ribbon embroidery stitches, instructions begin on page 8.

1. Make all desired ribbon pieces, such as flower, leaf, or bow. Mark placement on background, taking care to note which layer should be attached first, if necessary.

2. Tack ribbon piece on background, using small invisible stitches, like a slip stitch.

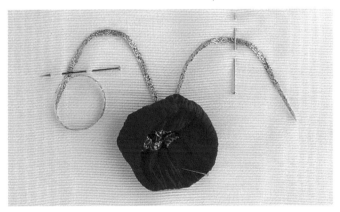

If you do not wish to make your own dimensional ribbon items, several companies offer pre-made ribbon flowers and bows for purchase. These can be found at most sewing, needlework, and crafts stores.

Silk, velvet, and lace flowers can also be appliquéd, using the dimensional ribbon technique. You can mix and match ribbon, silk, velvet, and lace flowers for an interesting design.

The ribbon flowers and motifs used in this book are described in the following instructions.

Cream Bud

Using a 4" piece of ⅝" creamy yellow wired satin ribbon, begin by folding over one end (A). Fold point over again (B) and stitch in place.

Continue folding—almost rolling—ribbon creating a spiraling tube (C). Complete bud by stitching end of ribbon to previously rolled section of tube (D).

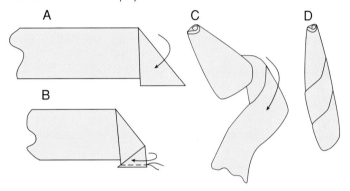

Birdhouse

Using a 1¾" piece of 1½" blue variegated satin ribbon, fold all sides under ¼" for a 1¼" x 1" rectangle (A). Position on fabric and tack in place.

Using a 1½" piece of ½" brown satin ribbon, fold in half. Mark the center on one side of fold. Unfold and fold top left and right corners down to center mark (where fold was). Trim ribbon so it is triangular shaped (B). Position "roof" on fabric, overlapping top edge of blue ribbon and tack in place.

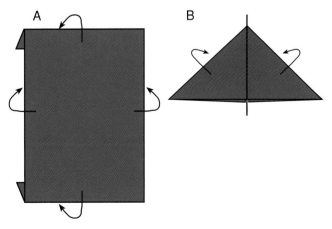

Fan

Cut eight 4¼" pieces of 1" teal and pink variegated satin ribbon. Begin at the left of the fan motif and fold ends of one ribbon piece under to fit the shape of fan (A). Position on fabric and tack ends in place (B). Repeat, working each ribbon piece individually to fit the shape of fan (C).

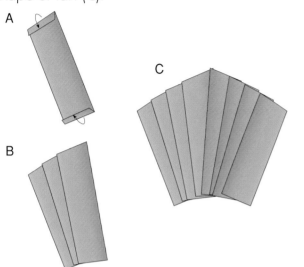

Fence

Using a 3¼" piece of ⅜" white grosgrain ribbon, fold both ends under ¼" (A). Fold left and right corners of one end toward center of ribbon and tack (B). Position on fabric and tack.

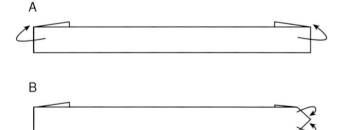

Folded Leaf

Cut three 6" pieces of 2" green organdy ribbon. Fold each as diagrammed. Sew a ¼" gathering stitch across bottom edges of each folded ribbon. Pull thread and wrap around ribbon twice. Knot and tack in place.

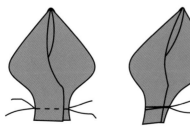

Large Daffodil

Cut six 3¼" pieces of ⅝" creamy yellow wired satin ribbon. Fold as diagrammed (A). Sew a ¼" gathering stitch across bottom edges of each folded ribbon. Pull thread and wrap around ribbon twice. Knot and tack in place on fabric.

Using a 14" piece of ⅝" yellow and orange variegated wired ribbon, fold ribbon in half lengthwise (B). Sew a gathering stitch along folded edge. Pull threads tightly to gather (C). Place in center of creamy yellow satin petals and tack in place.

Using a 6" piece of ⅝" yellow and orange variegated wired ribbon, fold in half with right sides together (D). Sew ¼" seam along short ends. Sew a gathering stitch along yellow edge (E). Position around gathered flower center, pull threads tightly and tack in place (F).

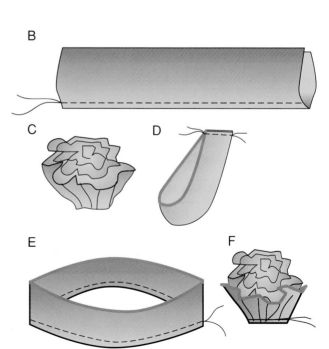

Large Pansy

For each Large Pansy, cut one 9" piece of ⅝" blue and purple variegated wired ribbon. Mark as indicated in diagram (A).

Fold ends forward at center marks (B). Sew a gathering stitch along outside edge as shown. Pull threads tightly to gather.

Stitch raw edges together to make pansy shape and secure thread (C). Position on design and tack in place with yellow Lazy Daisies.

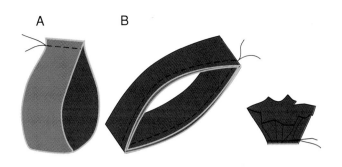

A

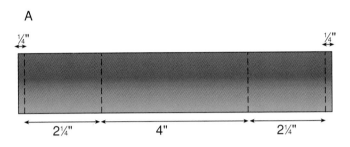

2¼"   4"   2¼"

B

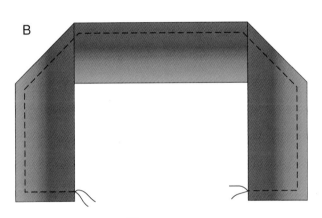

C

Large Poppy

For each Large Poppy, cut one 6" piece of ½" red with gold selvage wired ribbon. Fold in half with right sides together. Sew a ¼" seam along short ends (A).

Turn right side out and fold so selvage edges are together. Sew a gathering stitch along selvaged edge (B). Pull to gather. Tack in place.

Pansy Bud

For larger Pansy Bud, use a 9" piece of 1" teal and pink variegated ribbon and mark as indicated in Diagram A for Large Pansy.

For smaller Pansy Bud, use a 6" piece of 1" teal and pink variegated ribbon. Mark each as indicated in diagram below.

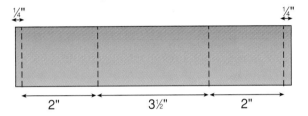

2"   3½"   2"

For each, fold ends forward at center marks as shown on Diagram B for Large Pansy. Sew a gathering stitch along outside edge as shown. Pull threads tightly to gather. Position on design and tack in place on its side.

Pink Heart

Using two 18" pieces of ½" pink pleated wired ribbon, sew short ends of ribbon together to make a 36" length. Sew a gathering stitch along one edge. Pull to gather. Place seam at bottom of heart and tack in place.

Pink Heart Folded Leaf

Cut three 6" pieces of 1" green satin ribbon. Fold each as diagrammed. Sew a ¼" gathering stitch across bottom edges of each folded ribbon. Pull thread and wrap around ribbon twice. Knot and tack in place.

Small Daffodil Center

Using a 4" piece of ⅝" yellow and orange variegated wired ribbon, begin at one end, folding end forward at right angle (A).

Fold vertical ribbon forward at right angle (B). Continue folding ribbon forward at right angles. Fold to center. Secure, leaving needle and thread attached.

Sew a gathering stitch on edge of remaining ribbon length (C). Gather tightly. Wrap gathered ribbon around folded ribbon.

Secure and fluff flower (D). Tack in place on its side.

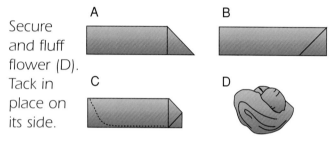

Small Folded Leaf

Cut three 5" pieces of 1" green organdy ribbon. Fold each as diagrammed. Sew a ¼" gathering stitch across bottom edges of each folded ribbon. Pull thread and wrap around ribbon twice. Knot and tack in place.

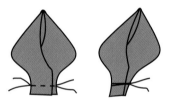

Small Poppy

Using a 10" piece of 13mm red silk ribbon, fold in half for a 5" length. Mark as indicated (A).

A

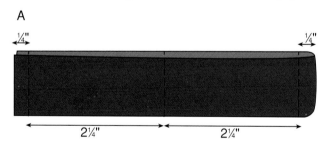

2¼"   2¼"

Fold 5" length at center mark and sew a gathering stitch as shown (B). Pull threads to gather (C). Tack in place.

B   C

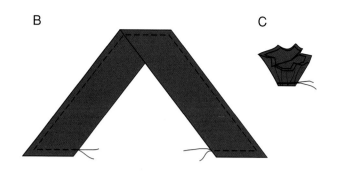

Rose

Using an 18" piece of 1½" cream organdy ribbon, sew a gathering stitch along ends and one long edge (A). Gather and tack in place.

Using an 18" piece of 2" pink satin ribbon, fold in half lengthwise (B). Sew a gathering stitch along one end and the selvage edge. Gather and tack in place on top of cream organdy.

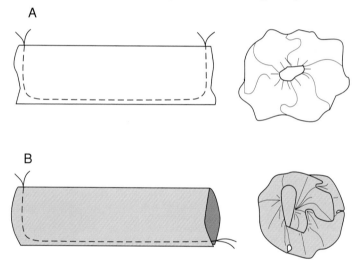

Tea Rosebud

Using a 4" piece of 1½" green, pink, and cream variegated wired ribbon, sew a gathering stitch along ends and one edge as shown (A). Pull threads to gather (B). Tuck gathers under and tack in place.

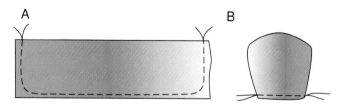

Tea Rose

Using two 18" lengths of 1½" green, pink, and cream variegated wired ribbon, place right sides together and sew a ¼" seam along one set of short ends (A).

Turn sewn ribbon and fold in half lengthwise (B). Sew a gathering stitch along ends and selvaged edges. Pull threads to gather and knot to secure.

A

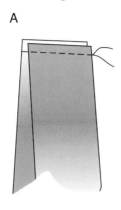

Wind gathered ribbon in a snail shell fashion, as diagrammed (C). Stitch bottom edges, as shown, to secure ribbon as a fully blossomed rose.

B

C

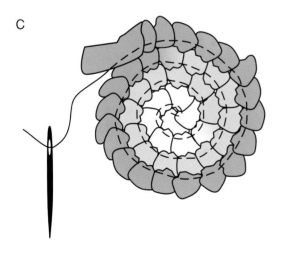

Wagon

Using a 3½" piece of 1" brown wired satin ribbon, fold ends under ½" for a 2½" rectangle. Position on fabric and tack in place.

Watering Can

Using a 2½" piece of 1½" silver metallic ribbon, fold ends under ¼" for a 2" x 1½" rectangle for can (A). Position on fabric and tack in place.

Using 1½" piece of 1½" silver metallic ribbon, fold right end under ¼" (B). From lower left corner, fold left end and lower edge of ribbon under as shown in the diagram. Trim ribbon so edges are not visible and to look like spout. Position on fabric, butting long left edge of spout to side of can and tack in place (C).

A   B   C

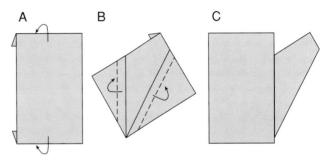

Painting Instructions

Painting on Fabric

Painting on fabric requires a textile medium. A textile medium is mixed with acrylic paint to make it glide better over fabric and permeate the fibers. It prevents paint from bleeding and makes the painting, when dry, permanent.

Fabric should be washed before painting and then ironed smooth. The fabric should then be stretched taut.

To use a textile medium, first pour a small amount of desired paint onto a palette. Place a few drops of medium onto paint. Mix well. The paint will become more transparent as more textile medium is added. Paint can also be diluted with water for a more transparent effect.

Paint. After the paint is dry, most fabrics painted with textile medium can be heat-set in a dryer or with a warm iron on the reverse side of fabric. Make certain to read and follow manufacturer's instructions when using a textile medium.

Rose Bud Bouquet

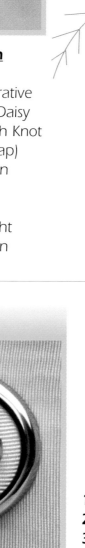

Ribbon/DMC Floss	Stitch
1 3346 floss (1 strand)	Stem
2 Dk. Red 4mm Silk	Decorative Lazy Daisy
3 Lt. Yellow 4mm Silk	French Knot (1 wrap)
4 Green 4mm Silk	Ribbon
5 3346 floss (1 strand)	Leaf
6 White 7mm Silk	Loop
7 White 7mm Silk	Straight
8 White 7mm Silk	Ribbon

Pinecones

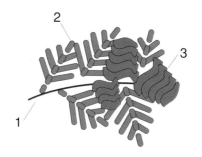

Ribbon/DMC Floss	Stitch
1 3031 floss (6 strands)	Stem
2 Dk. Green 4mm Silk	Leaf
3 Gold 4mm Silk tacked with 729 floss (1 strand)	Pinecone

Tulips

Ribbon/DMC Floss	Stitch
1 Dk. Green 4mm Silk	Whipped Running
2 White 4mm Silk	Decorative Lazy Daisy
3 Dk. Red 4mm Silk	Decorative Lazy Daisy
4 Button	Beading
5 Dk. Green 4mm Silk couched with 501 floss (1 strand)	Couched

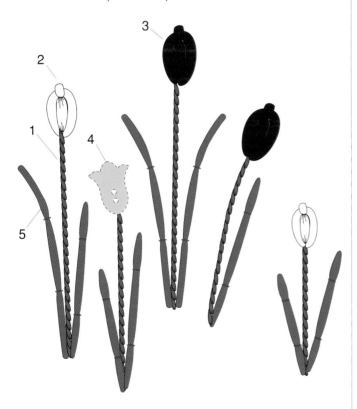

Purple Rose

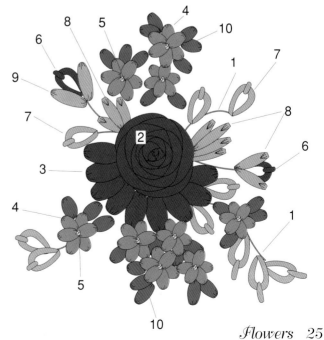

Ribbon/DMC Floss	Stitch
1 3364 floss (1 strand)	Stem
2 Purple 4mm Silk	Spider Web Rose
3 Purple 4mm Silk	Straight
4 Lt. Purple 4mm Silk	Straight
5 3609 floss (3 strands)	French Knot (2 wraps)
6 Purple 4mm Silk	Lazy Daisy
7 Lt. Green 4mm Silk	Lazy Daisy
8 Lt. Green 4mm Silk	Ribbon
9 Lt. Green 4mm Silk	Straight
10 Dk. Green 4mm Silk	Straight

Pansies & Diamonds

	Ribbon/DMC Floss	Stitch
1	3364 floss (1 strand)	Chain
2	Lt. Blue 4mm Silk	Straight
3	Mauve 4mm Silk	Ribbon
4	Lt. Yellow 4mm Silk	Straight
5	310 floss (1 strand)	Straight
6	Dk. Green 4mm Silk	Lazy Daisy

Additional Designs

Birds of Paradise Border

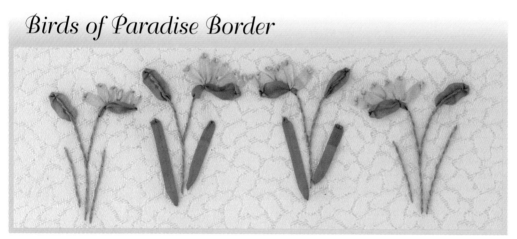

	Ribbon/DMC Floss	Stitch		Ribbon/DMC Floss	Stitch
1	Lt. Green 4mm Silk	Ribbon	4	Lt. Pink 4mm Silk	Ribbon
2	Green 4mm Silk	Straight	5	Lt. Blue 4mm Silk	Ribbon
3	3347 floss (2 strands)	Stem	6	341 floss (2 strands)	Straight

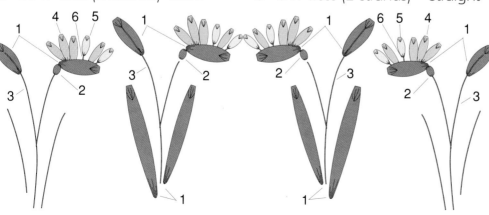

Blue Baby's Breath

Ribbon/DMC Floss	Stitch
1 3348 floss (1 strand)	Stem
2 White 4mm Silk	Padded Straight
3 Lt. Green 4mm Silk	Straight
4 Pale Blue 7mm Silk	Loop
5 Pale Blue 7mm Silk	Loose Running

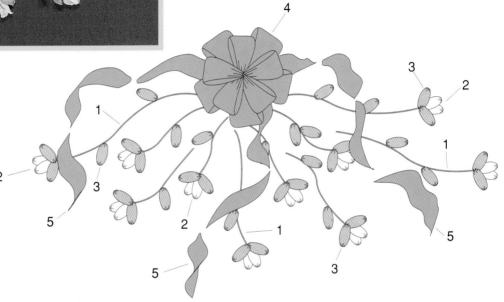

Lavender Heart

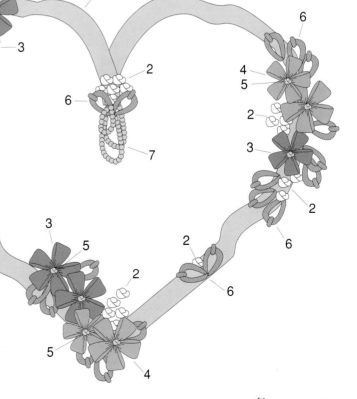

Ribbon/DMC Floss	Stitch
1 Lavender 16mm Organdy	Tacked Ribbon
2 Off-white 4mm Silk	French Knot (1 wrap)
3 Purple 4mm Silk	Loop
4 Rose 4mm Silk	Loop
5 738 floss (1 strand)	French Knot (3 wraps)
6 Lt. Green 4mm Silk	Lazy Daisy
7 Lavender Beads	Bead Stringing

Rose Half Wreath

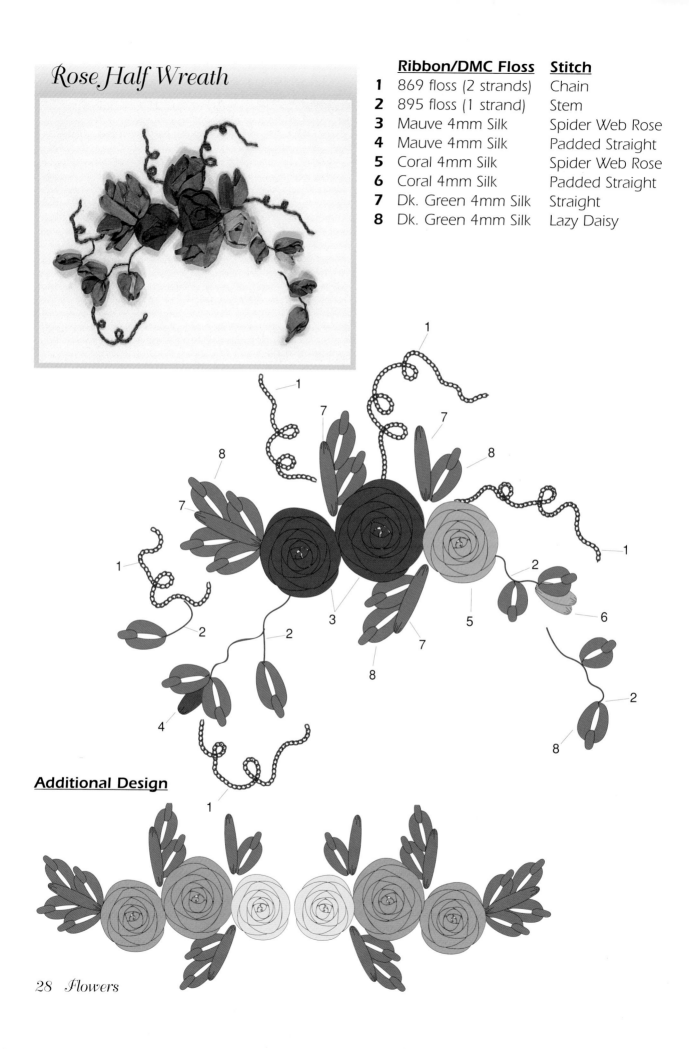

	Ribbon/DMC Floss	Stitch
1	869 floss (2 strands)	Chain
2	895 floss (1 strand)	Stem
3	Mauve 4mm Silk	Spider Web Rose
4	Mauve 4mm Silk	Padded Straight
5	Coral 4mm Silk	Spider Web Rose
6	Coral 4mm Silk	Padded Straight
7	Dk. Green 4mm Silk	Straight
8	Dk. Green 4mm Silk	Lazy Daisy

Additional Design

Sunflower & Dragonflies

Ribbon/DMC Floss		Stitch
1	Lt. Yellow 7mm Silk	Ribbon
2	Brown 4mm Silk	French Knot (2 wraps)
3	Dk. Green 4mm Silk	Whipped Running
4	Green 4mm Silk	Leaf
5	319 floss (1 strand)	Stem
6	Brown 4mm Silk	Whipped Running
7	Gold 4mm Silk	Straight
8	782 floss (1 strand)	Pistil
9	Aqua 4mm Silk	Straight
10	Teal 4mm Silk	Straight
11	Bright Yellow 4mm Silk	Straight
12	501 floss (1 strand)	French Knot (2 wraps)

Additional Design

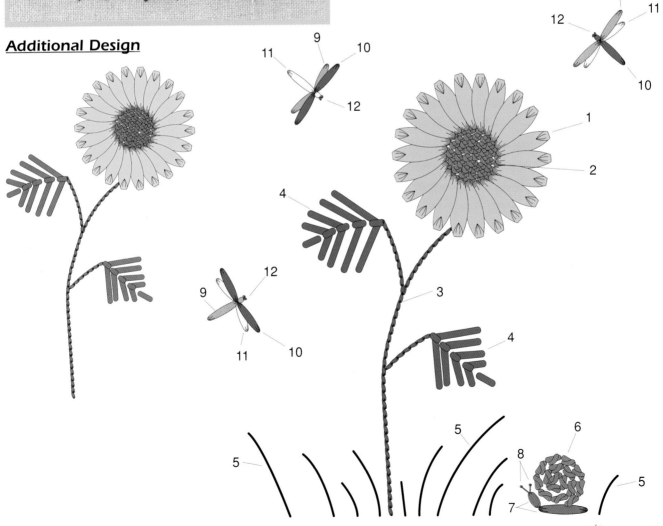

Purple Basket

	Ribbon/DMC Floss	**Stitch**
1	902 floss (2 strands)	Chain
2	902 floss (2 strands)	Stem
3	Mauve 4mm Silk	Ribbon
4	Lt. Blue 4mm Silk	Straight
5	Lt. Yellow 4mm Silk	Straight
6	310 floss (1 strand)	Straight
7	Bright Yellow 4mm Silk	Straight
8	310 floss (1 strand)	French Knot (3 wraps)
9	3345 floss (1 strand)	Stem
10	Purple 4mm Silk	French Knot (1 wrap)
11	White 4mm Silk	French Knot (1 wrap)
12	Blue 4mm Silk	French Knot (1 wrap)
13	Lavender 4mm Silk	French Knot (1 wrap)
14	Dk. Green 4mm Silk	Lazy Daisy
15	Yellow 4mm Silk	Straight

	Ribbon/DMC Floss	**Stitch**
16	310 floss (3 strands)	Straight
17	310 floss (3 strands)	French Knot (1 wrap)
18	Lt. Yellow 4mm Silk	Straight

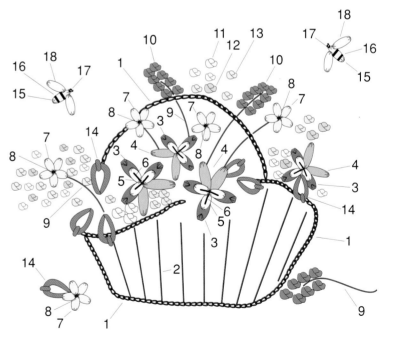

Hummingbird

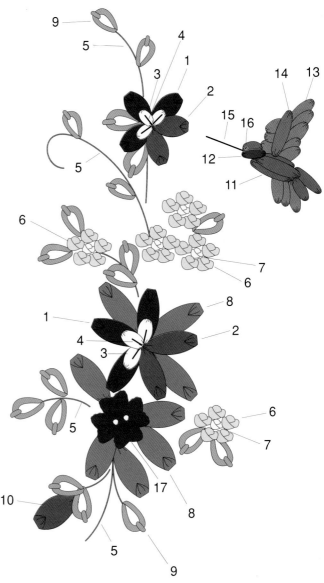

	Ribbon/DMC Floss	Stitch
1	Purple 7mm Silk	Ribbon
2	Mauve 7mm Silk	Ribbon
3	Lt. Yellow 4mm Silk	Straight
4	310 floss (1 strand)	Straight
5	988 floss (2 strands)	Stem
6	Med. Blue 4mm Silk	French Knot (2 wraps)
7	Bright Yellow 4mm Silk	French Knot (2 wraps)
8	Dk. Green 7mm Silk	Ribbon
9	Bright Green 4mm Silk	Lazy Daisy
10	Mauve 4mm Silk	Ribbon
11	Blue-green 4mm Silk	Straight
12	Red 4mm Silk	Straight
13	Brown 4mm Silk	Straight
14	Gold 4mm Silk	Straight
15	310 floss (1 strand)	Straight
16	310 floss (1 strand)	French Knot (3 wraps)
17	Button	Beading

Additional Designs

Pink & Purple

	Ribbon/DMC Floss	Stitch
1	895 floss (1 strand)	Stem
2	966 floss (1 strand)	Stem
3	Lt. Purple 4mm Silk	Ribbon
4	Dusty Rose 4mm Silk	French Knot (1 wrap)
5	Bright Rose 4mm Silk	French Knot (1 wrap)
6	3687 floss (1 strand)	French Knot (2 wraps)
7	Lt. Purple 4mm Silk	Straight
8	Teal 4mm Silk	Straight
9	Lt. Green 4mm Silk	Straight

Additional Design

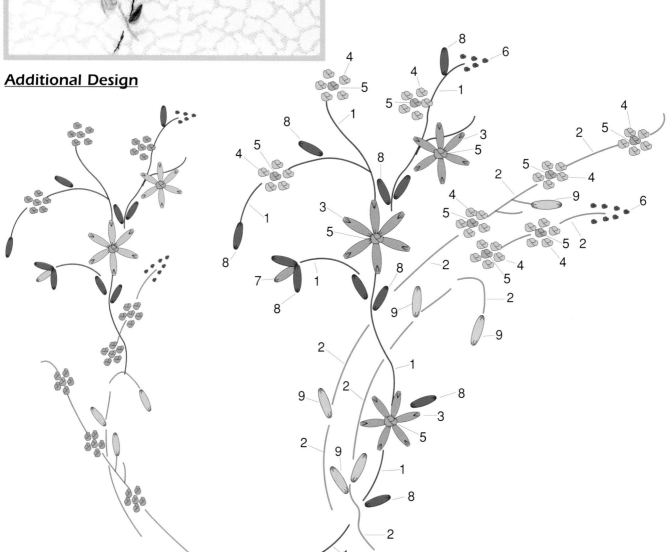

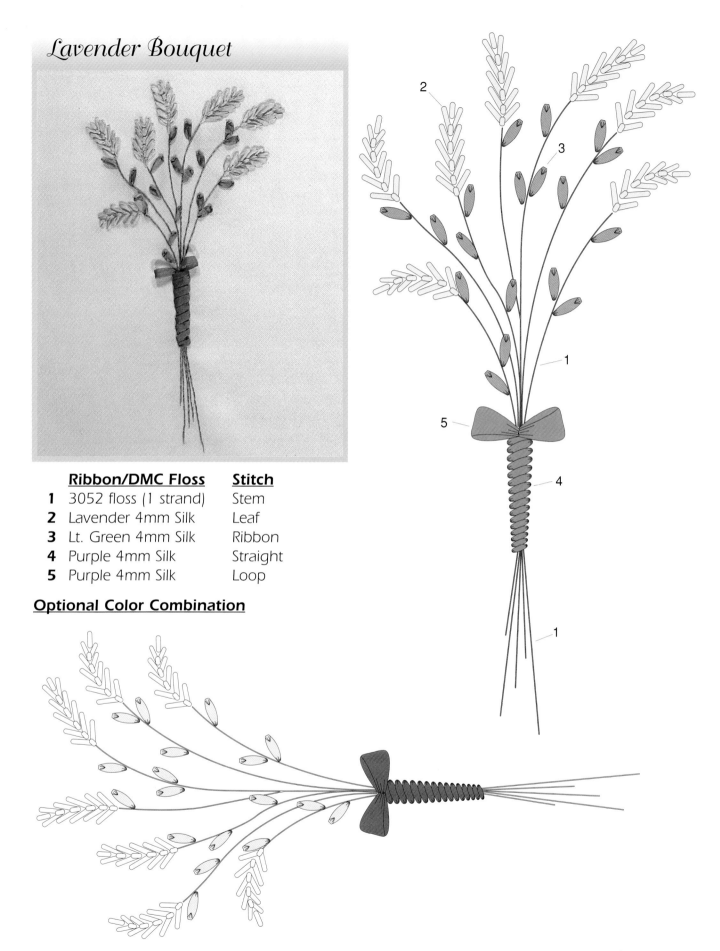

Lavender Bouquet

Ribbon/DMC Floss	Stitch
1 3052 floss (1 strand)	Stem
2 Lavender 4mm Silk	Leaf
3 Lt. Green 4mm Silk	Ribbon
4 Purple 4mm Silk	Straight
5 Purple 4mm Silk	Loop

Optional Color Combination

Sunflower Spray

	Ribbon/DMC Floss	Stitch		Ribbon/DMC Floss	Stitch
1	Gold 4mm Silk	Woven Ribbon	**7**	Lt. Green 4mm Silk	Lazy Daisy
2	Yellow 7mm Silk	Ribbon	**8**	Lt. Yellow 4mm Silk	Ribbon
3	Yellow-gold 4mm Silk	Ribbon	**9**	White 4mm Silk	Straight
4	Yellow-gold 4mm Silk	Stem	**10**	Bright Yellow 4mm Silk	French Knot
5	Dk. Green 4mm Silk	Straight			(2 wraps)
6	Gold 4mm Silk	Stem			

Additional Designs

Lilies

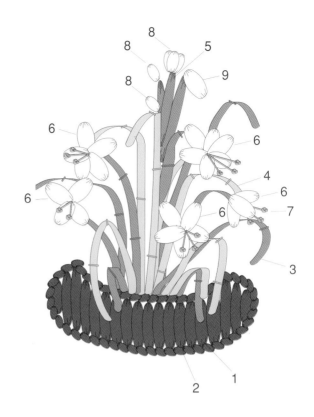

	Ribbon/DMC Floss	Stitch
1	Purple 4mm Silk	Satin
2	Purple 4mm Silk	Stem
3	Dk. Green 4mm Silk couched with 319 floss (1 strand)	Couched
4	Lt. Green 4mm Silk couched with 955 floss (1 strand)	Couched

	Ribbon/DMC Floss	Stitch
5	Dk. Green 4mm Silk	Straight
6	White 7mm Silk	Straight
7	3326 floss (3 strands)	Pistil
8	White 4mm Silk	Straight
9	White 4mm Silk	Padded Straight

Optional Color Combination & Additional Design

What a difference a flower makes

Bordered Daisies

	Ribbon/DMC Floss	Stitch
1	White 7mm Silk	Lazy Daisy
2	Bright Yellow 4mm Silk	French Knot (3 wraps)
3	Lt. Yellow 4mm Silk	French Knot (1 wrap)
4	White 4mm Silk	Lazy Daisy
5	Bright Yellow 4mm Silk	French Knot (2 wraps)
6	Green 4mm Silk	Ribbon
7	Lt. Green 4mm Silk	Lazy Daisy
8	Lt. Yellow 4mm Silk	Coral

Additional Design

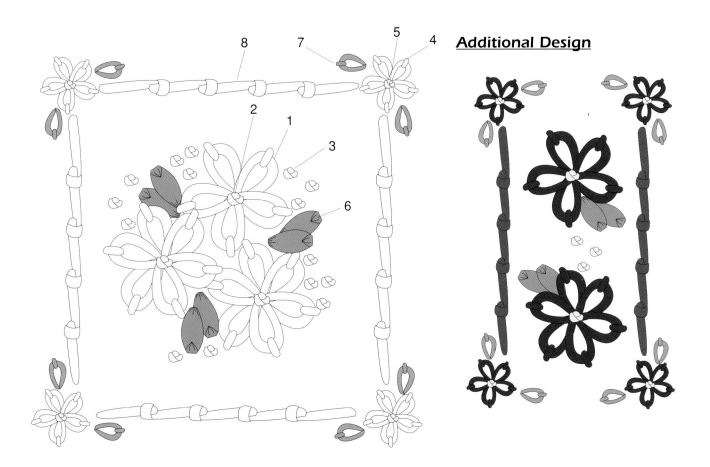

Scattered Roses

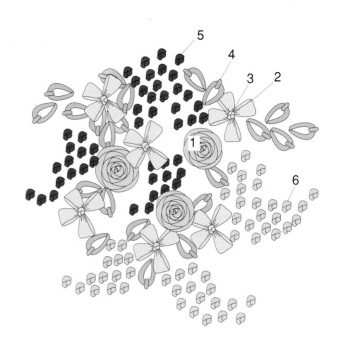

Ribbon/DMC Floss	Stitch
1 Pink 4mm Silk	Spider Web Rose
2 Lt. Yellow 4mm Silk	Loop
3 Dk. Yellow 4mm Silk	French Knot (1 wrap)
4 Lt. Green 4mm Silk	Lazy Daisy

Ribbon/DMC Floss	Stitch
5 Maroon 4mm Silk	French Knot (1 wrap)
6 Pink 4mm Silk	French Knot (1 wrap)

Optional Color Combination & Additional Design

Plant happy thoughts deep in your heart And watch a garden of memories start.

Bleeding Heart

Ribbon/DMC Floss	Stitch
1 Mauve 4mm Silk woven with Lt. Blue 4mm Silk	Woven Running
2 Mauve 4mm Silk	Straight
3 Mauve 4mm Silk Pink 4mm Silk	Spider Web Rose
4 Blue 4mm Silk	Bullion Lazy Daisy
5 Pink 4mm Silk	Lazy Daisy
6 Lt. Green 4mm Silk	Stem
7 Lt. Green 4mm Silk	Straight
8 Lt. Green 4mm Silk	Ribbon
9 Lt. Green 4mm Silk	Lazy Daisy
10 Pink Beads	Beading

Additional Designs

Lilacs

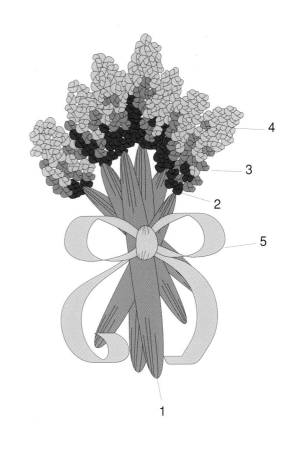

Ribbon/DMC Floss		Stitch
1	Green 4mm Silk	Straight
2	Dk. Purple 4mm Silk	French Knot (1 wrap)
3	Purple 4mm Silk	French Knot (1 wrap)

Ribbon/DMC Floss		Stitch
4	Lavender 4mm Silk	French Knot (1 wrap)
5	Yellow 4mm Silk	Bow—Tacking

Optional Color Combination & Additional Design

Lilacs
whisper
of
Love's first emotions

Small Pastel Wreath

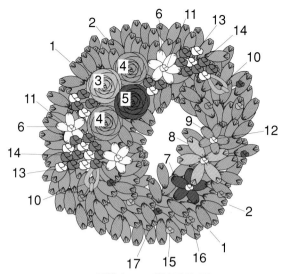

	Ribbon/DMC Floss	Stitch
1	Dk Green 4mm Silk	Ribbon
2	Lt. Green 4mm Silk	Ribbon
3	Peach 4mm Silk	Spider Web Rose
4	Mauve 4mm Silk	Spider Web Rose
5	Maroon 4mm Silk	Spider Web Rose
6	Lt. Yellow 4mm Silk	Straight
7	Maroon 4mm Silk	Straight
8	Peach 4mm Silk	Ribbon
9	Mauve 4mm Silk	Straight
10	Peach 4mm Silk	Lazy Daisy
11	White 4mm Silk	French Knot (1 wrap)

	Ribbon/DMC Floss	Stitch
11	Lt. Yellow 4mm Silk	French Knot (1 wrap)
12	White 4mm Silk	French Knot (2 wraps)
13	Purple 4mm Silk	French Knot (2 wraps)
14	Peach 4mm Silk	French Knot (2 wraps)
15	Mauve 4mm Silk	French Knot (2 wraps)
16	Maroon 4mm Silk	French Knot (2 wraps)

Pink Bow & Roses

	Ribbon/DMC Floss	Stitch
1	Pink 7mm Silk	Tacked Ribbon
	tacked with	French Knot (1 wrap)
2	Pink 4mm Silk	Loop
3	Pink 4mm Silk	Straight
4	Peach 4mm Silk	Spider Web Rose
5	Lt. Peach 4mm Silk	Spider Web Rose
6	Lt. Green 4mm Silk	Lazy Daisy

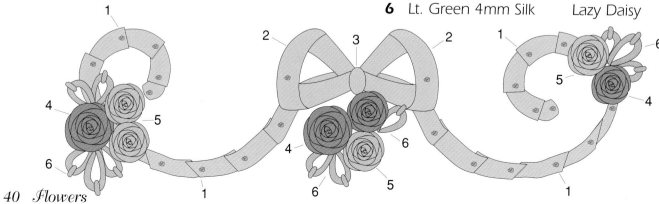

Radish

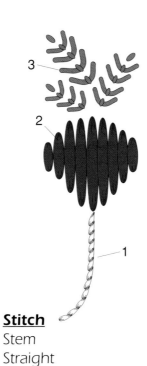

Ribbon/DMC Floss	Stitch
1 White 4mm Silk	Stem
2 Red 4mm Silk	Straight
3 Green 4mm Silk	Leaf

Broccoli

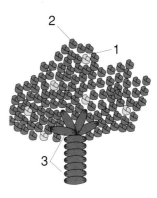

Ribbon/DMC Floss	Stitch
1 Yellow 4mm Silk	French Knot (1 wrap)
2 Dk. Green 4mm Silk	French Knot (1 wrap)
3 Green 4mm Silk	Straight

Pumpkin Patch

Ribbon/DMC Floss	Stitch
1 Orange 7mm Silk couched with 947 floss (1 strand)	Couched
2 Brown 4mm Silk	Straight
3 434 floss (2 strands)	Stem
4 310 floss (1 strand)	Straight
5 Green 4mm Silk	Straight
6 904 floss (1 strand)	Stem

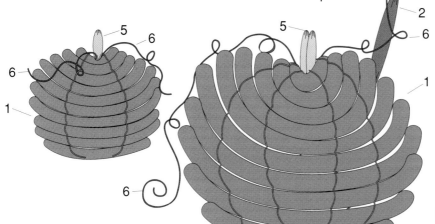

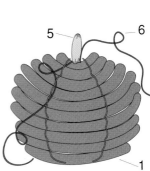

Red Peppers

	Ribbon/DMC Floss	Stitch
1	Red 4mm Silk	Satin
2	Green 4mm Silk	Ribbon
3	Green 4mm Silk	Straight
4	Off-white 4mm Silk	Twisted Straight
5	Off-white 4mm Silk	Loop
6	Off-white 4mm Silk	Straight

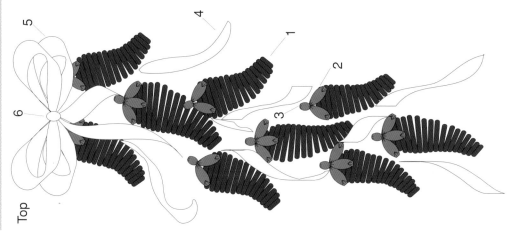

Pineapple

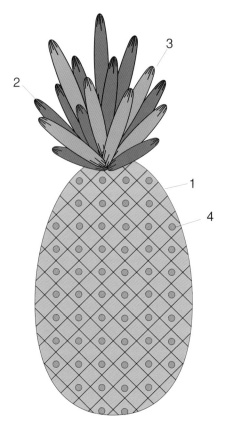

	Ribbon/DMC Floss	Stitch
1	Yellow 4mm Silk	Woven Ribbon
2	Dk. Green 4mm Silk	Straight
3	Lt. Green 4mm Silk	Straight
4	Gold Beads	Beading

Grape Basket

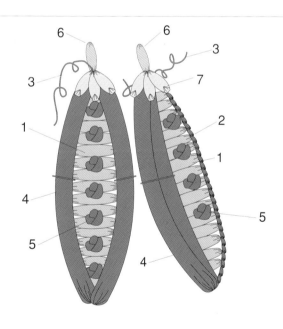

	Ribbon/DMC Floss	Stitch
1	Silver Metallic #16	Whipped Running
2	Silver Metallic #16	Couched
3	Silver Metallic #16 (double strands)	Straight
4	Dk. Purple 4mm Silk	French Knot (2 wraps)

	Ribbon/DMC Floss	Stitch
5	Lt. Purple 4mm Silk	French Knot (2 wraps)
6	3348 floss (1 strand)	Chain
7	Lt. Green 4mm Silk	Lazy Daisy

Sweet Peas

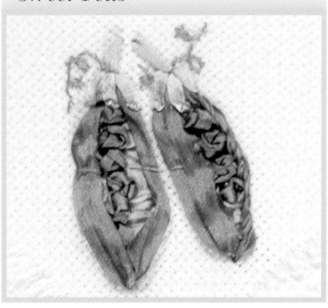

	Ribbon/DMC Floss	Stitch
1	Lt. Green 4mm Silk	Straight
2	Dk. Green 7mm Silk	Stem
3	471 floss (1 strand)	Stem
4	Dk. Green 7mm Silk couched with 471 floss (1 strand)	Couched

	Ribbon/DMC Floss	Stitch
5	Dk. Green 7mm Silk	French Knot (2 wraps)
6	Lt. Green 4mm Silk	Straight
7	Lt. Yellow 4mm Silk	Ribbon

Lettuce Heads

	Ribbon/DMC Floss	Stitch
1	Lt. Green 4mm Silk	Spider Web Rose
	Dk. Green 7mm Silk	
2	Dk. Green 7mm Silk	Ribbon

Top

Watermelon

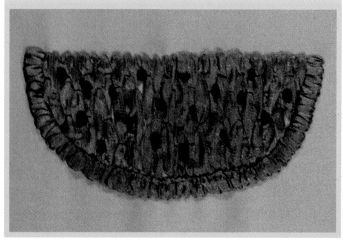

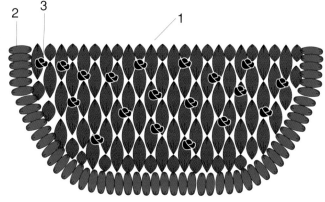

	Ribbon/DMC Floss	Stitch
1	Mauve 4mm Silk	Satin
2	Dk. Green 4mm Silk	Straight
3	Black 4mm Silk	French Knot (1 wrap)

Optional Color Combination

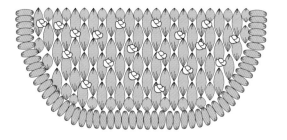

Strawberries

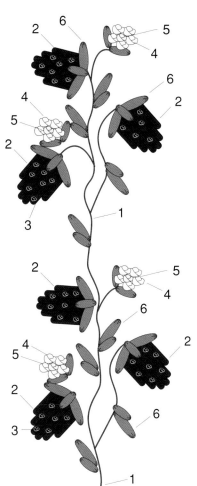

	Ribbon/DMC Floss	Stitch
1	3345 floss (2 strands)	Stem
2	Red 4mm Silk	Satin
3	310 floss (1 strand)	French Knot (1 wrap)
4	Off-white 4mm Silk	French Knot (1 wrap)
5	Yellow 4mm Silk	French Knot (1 wrap)
6	Green 4mm Silk	Straight

Optional Color Combination

Grapevine

	Ribbon/DMC Floss	Stitch
1	Dk. Purple 4mm Silk	French Knot (1 wrap)
2	Lt. Purple 4mm Silk	French Knot (1 wrap)
3	Dk. Green 4mm Silk	Whipped Running
4	Dk. Green 4mm Silk	Lazy Daisy
5	Lt. Green 7mm Silk	Running

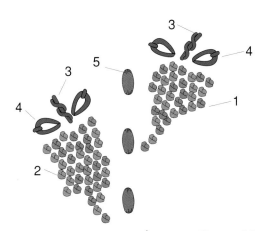

Apple Bushel

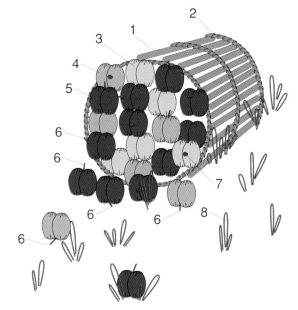

Ribbon/DMC Floss		Stitch
1	Brown 4mm Silk	Straight
2	Brown 4mm Silk	Stem
3	Yellow 4mm Silk	Straight
4	Green 4mm Silk	Straight
5	Red 4mm Silk	Straight

Ribbon/DMC Floss		Stitch
6	801 floss (1 strand)	Straight
7	801 floss (1 strand)	French Knot (1 wrap)
8	895 floss (1 strand)	Lazy Daisy

Ear of Corn

Ribbon/DMC Floss		Stitch
1	Yellow 7mm Silk couched with 745 floss (1 strand)	Couched
2	Dk. Green 7mm Silk	Straight
3	895 floss (1 strand)	Backstitch

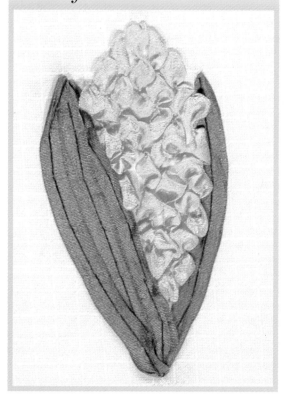

Optional Color Combination

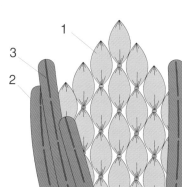

Cherries

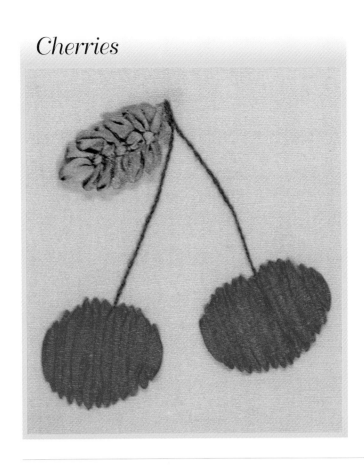

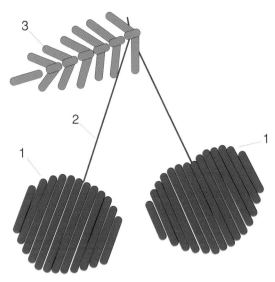

Ribbon/DMC Floss	Stitch
1 Red 4mm Silk	Satin
2 801 floss (2 strands)	Stem
3 Green 4mm Silk	Leaf

Grape Cluster

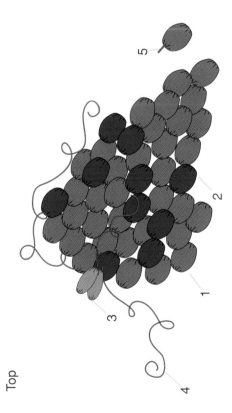

Top

Ribbon/DMC Floss	Stitch
1 Mauve 4mm Silk	Padded Straight
2 Maroon 4mm Silk	Padded Straight
3 Brown 4mm Silk	Straight
4 3345 floss (1 strand)	Stem
5 3345 floss (1 strand)	Straight

Shamrocks

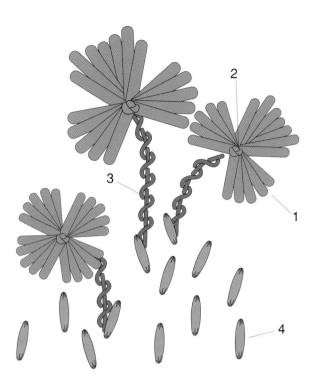

Ribbon/DMC Floss	Stitch
1 Med. Green 4mm Silk	Straight
2 Med. Green 4mm Silk	French Knot (1 wrap)

Ribbon/DMC Floss	Stitch
3 Dk. Green 4mm Silk	Whipped Running
4 Lt. Green 4mm Silk	Straight

Raspberries

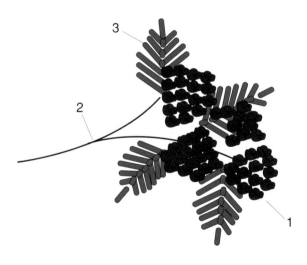

Ribbon/DMC Floss	Stitch
1 Red 4mm Silk	French Knot (1 wrap)
2 801 floss (3 strands)	Stem
3 Dk. Green 4mm Silk	Leaf

Butterfly Border

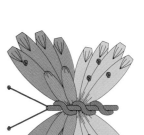

	Ribbon/DMC Floss	Stitch
1	Dusty Purple 4mm Silk	Whipped Running
2	Lavender 7mm Silk	Ribbon
3	Lt. Pink 7mm Silk	Ribbon
4	Lt. Blue 4mm Silk	Straight
5	3041 floss (2 strands)	French Knot (2 wraps)
6	3041 floss (2 strands)	Pistil
7	Lt. Green 4mm Silk	Lazy Daisy
8	Rose 4mm Silk	Ribbon
9	Rose 4mm Silk	Straight
10	Lt. Yellow 4mm Silk	French Knot (1 wrap)

Inchworm

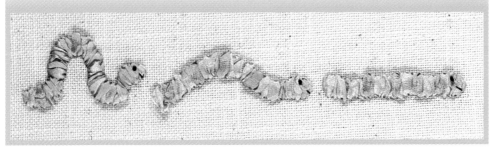

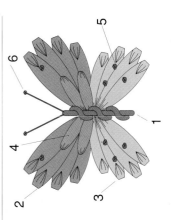

	Ribbon/DMC Floss	Stitch
1	Lt. Green 4mm Silk	Satin
2	Dk. Green 4mm Silk	Straight
3	310 floss (1 strand)	French Knot (1 wrap)
4	310 floss (1 strand)	Straight

Top

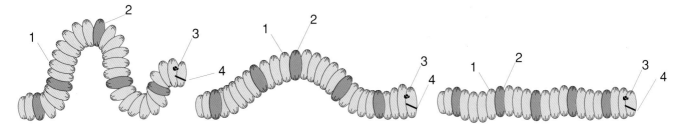

Sunflower Fence

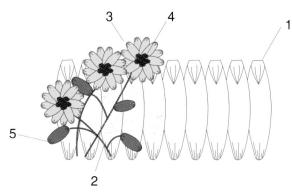

	Ribbon/DMC Floss	Stitch
1	White 7mm Silk	Ribbon
2	561 floss (2 strands)	Outline
3	Yellow 4mm Silk	Straight
4	801 floss (6 strands)	French Knot (1 wrap)
5	Dk. Green 7mm Silk	Straight

Unicorn

	Ribbon/DMC Floss	Stitch
1	White 4mm Silk couched with White floss (1 strand)	Couched
2	310 floss (1 strand)	Stem
3	Black 4mm Silk	French Knot (1 wrap)
4	Gold Med. Braid	Straight
5	Gold Med. Braid	Satin
6	Lt. Blue 4mm Silk	Twisted Straight
7	Dk. Blue 4mm Silk	Stem Rose
8	Green 4mm Silk	Lazy Daisy

Additional Design

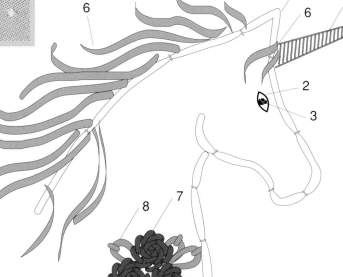

Wedding Bells

Ribbon/DMC Floss / Stitch

#	Ribbon/DMC Floss	Stitch
1	Lt. Blue 4mm Silk	Stem
2	Dusty Rose 4mm Silk	Coral
3	Salmon 4mm Silk	Spider Web Rose
4	Yellow 4mm Silk	Ribbon
5	955 floss (2 strands)	Stem
6	Lt. Green 4mm Silk	Ribbon
7	Dk. Green 4mm Silk	Ribbon
8	Yellow Beads	Beading
9	Lt. Blue 4mm Silk	Couched
	Med. Blue 4mm Silk couched with 3755 floss (1 strand)	
10	Lt. Blue 4mm Silk	Straight

Additional Design

Spring Hatrack

	Ribbon/DMC Floss	Stitch
1	Off-white 7mm Silk	Woven Ribbon
2	Off-white 7mm Silk	Straight
3	Pink 4mm Silk	Backstitch
4	Yellow 4mm Silk	Ribbon
5	Green 4mm Silk	Ribbon
6	Lt. Blue 4mm Silk	French Knot (1 wrap)
7	Med. Blue 4mm Silk	French Knot (1 wrap)
8	Brown 4mm Silk	French Knot (1 wrap)
9	Gold 4mm Silk	Whipped Running
10	Gold 4mm Silk	Stem
11	Gold 4mm Silk	French Knot (3 wraps)
12	Off-white 4mm Silk	Loop
	Pink 4mm Silk	
13	Off-white 4mm Silk	Couched
	Pink 4mm Silk	
	couched with	
	963 floss (1 strand)	

Country Mailbox

	Ribbon/DMC Floss	Stitch
1	Brown 4mm Silk	Straight
2	Off-white 4mm Silk	Satin
3	451 floss (2 strands)	Stem
4	3345 floss (2 strands)	Stem
5	Dk. Green 4mm Silk	Ribbon
6	Rose 4mm Silk	Ribbon
7	Rose 4mm Silk	Straight
8	702 floss (2 strands)	Stem
9	Green 4mm Silk	Straight
10	Lt. Purple 4mm Silk	Plume
11	904 floss (1 strand)	Straight
12	Yellow 4mm Silk	French Knot (1 wrap)
13	Brown 4mm Silk	Padded Straight
14	Salmon 4mm Silk	Lazy Daisy
15	725 floss (1 strand)	Pistil
16	Red 4mm Silk	Straight

Additional Design

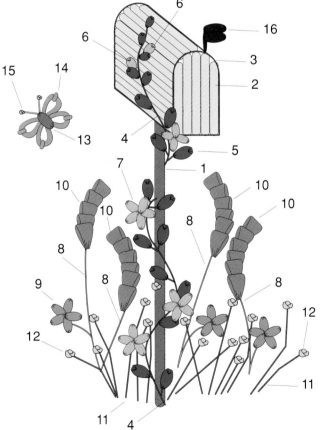

Sheep to Sheep

Ribbon/DMC Floss   Stitch

	Ribbon/DMC Floss	Stitch
1	838 floss (6 strands)	Decorative Lazy Daisy
2	White 4mm Silk	Loose Straight
3	Off-white 7mm Silk	Loose Straight
4	Lt. Yellow 4mm Silk	Loose Straight
5	Lt. Green 4mm Silk	Straight
6	Green 4mm Silk	Straight
7	Dk. Green 4mm Silk	Straight

Additional Design

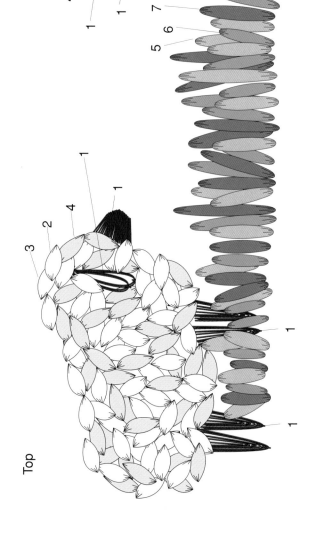

Top

Carousel Horse

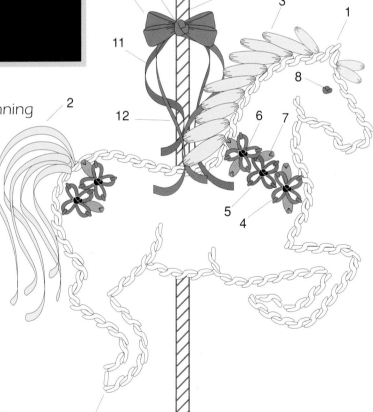

	Ribbon/DMC Floss	Stitch
1	White 4mm Silk	Whipped Running
2	Yellow 4mm Silk couched with 739 floss (1 strand)	Couched
3	Yellow 4mm Silk	Straight
4	Rose 4mm Silk	Lazy Daisy
5	Med. Blue 4mm Silk	Lazy Daisy
6	Black 4mm Silk	French Knot (2 wraps)
7	Green 4mm Silk	Ribbon
8	Gold 4mm Silk	French Knot (2 wraps)
9	782 floss (1 strand) Gold Med. Braid	Stem
10	782 floss (1 strand) Gold Med. Braid	Straight
11	Med. Blue 4mm Silk	Tacked Ribbon
12	Rose 4mm Silk	Tacked Ribbon
13	Rose 4mm Silk	Loop
14	Rose 4mm Silk	French Knot (2 wraps)

Mantel Clock

Ribbon/DMC Floss	Stitch		Ribbon/DMC Floss	Stitch
1 Maroon 4mm Silk	Whipped Running	**8**	Brown Beads	Beading
2 902 floss (2 strands)	Chain	**9**	890 floss (1 strand)	Stem
3 310 floss (1 strand)	Straight	**10**	Gold 13mm Silk	Spider Web Rose
4 310 floss (1 strand)	Stem	**11**	Gold 4mm Silk	Spider Web Rose
5 Black 4mm Silk	Straight	**12**	Gold 4mm Silk	Lazy Daisy
6 Black 4mm Silk	French Knot (2 wraps)	**13**	Green 4mm Silk	Ribbon
7 Gold 13mm Silk	Folded Rose	**14**	Green 4mm Silk	Lazy Daisy

Carrot Bunny

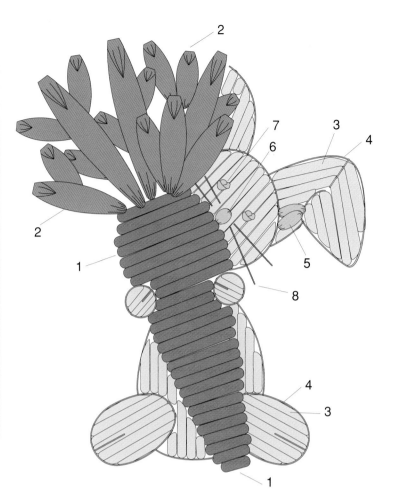

	Ribbon/DMC Floss	Stitch
1	Orange 4mm Silk	Satin
2	Green 4mm Silk	Ribbon
3	Lt. Yellow 4mm Silk	Satin
4	436 floss (3 strands)	Stem
5	Pink 4mm Silk	Straight
6	Pink 4mm Silk	Padded Straight
7	Med. Blue 4mm Silk	French Knot (3 wraps)
8	415 floss (3 strands)	Straight

Additional Design

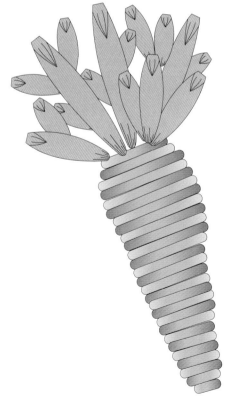

Additional Design

Gingerbread Man

	Ribbon/DMC Floss	Stitch		Ribbon/DMC Floss	Stitch
1	Brown 4mm Silk	Whipped Running	**11**	Dk. Brown 4mm Silk	Straight
2	Brown 4mm Silk	Whipped Running	**12**	Gray 4mm Silk couched with White floss (1 strand)	Couched
3	Brown 4mm Silk	Straight			
4	Brown 4mm Silk	Straight			
5	Brown 4mm Silk	Straight	**13**	Yellow 4mm Silk	Woven Ribbon
6	310 floss (1 strand)	French Knot (1 wrap)	**14**	Yellow 4mm Silk	Straight
			15	White floss (1 strand)	French Knot (1 wrap)
7	310 floss (1 strand)	Straight			
8	310 floss (1 strand)	Straight	**16**	310 floss (1 strand)	Backstitch
9	Gray 4mm Silk	French Knot (1 to 3 wraps)	**17**	310 floss (1 strand)	French Knot (1 wrap)
10	Dk. Green 4mm Silk	Leaf	**18**	Button	Beading

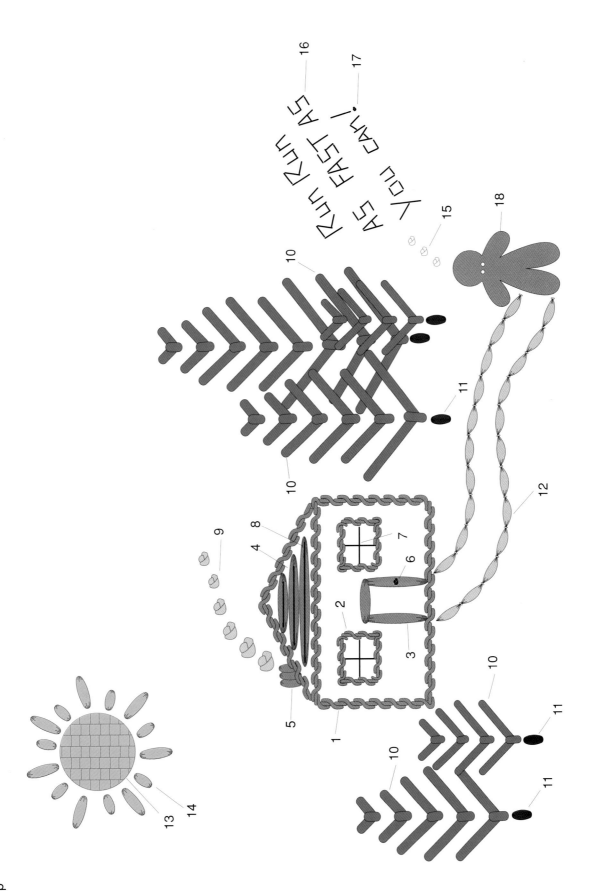

RUN RUN RUN
AS FAST AS
YOU CAN!

Top

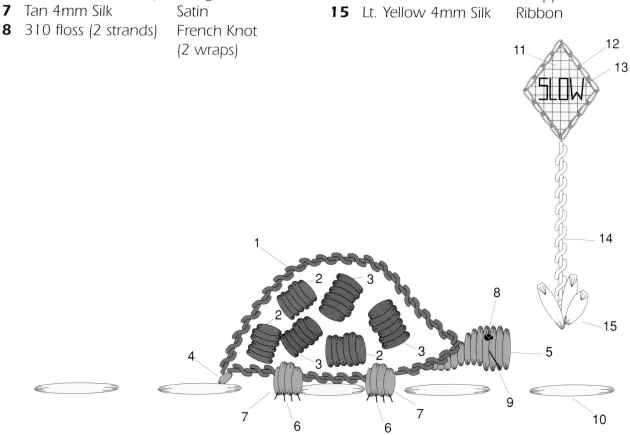

	Ribbon/DMC Floss	Stitch		Ribbon/DMC Floss	Stitch
1	Brown 4mm Silk	Whipped Running	**9**	310 floss (2 strands)	Stem
2	Brown 4mm Silk	Satin	**10**	Yellow 4mm Silk	Straight
3	Gold 4mm Silk	Satin	**11**	Yellow 4mm Silk	Woven Ribbon
4	Tan 4mm Silk	Straight	**12**	445 floss (1 strand)	Chain
5	Tan 4mm Silk	Satin	**13**	310 floss (1 strand)	Backstitch
6	310 floss (2 strands)	Straight	**14**	White 4mm Silk	Whipped Running
7	Tan 4mm Silk	Satin	**15**	Lt. Yellow 4mm Silk	Ribbon
8	310 floss (2 strands)	French Knot (2 wraps)			

Butterfly Basket

Ribbon/DMC Floss		Stitch
1	Blue 4mm Silk	Chain
2	Blue 4mm Silk	Whipped Running
3	Lt. Blue 4mm Silk	Woven Ribbon
4	Maroon 4mm Silk	Free Form Flower
5	Mauve 4mm Silk	Free Form Flower
6	Maroon 4mm Silk	Ribbon
7	Dk. Green 4mm Silk	Lazy Daisy
8	Lt. Green 4mm Silk	Ribbon
9	Pink Beads	Beading
10	Off-white 4mm Silk	French Knot (1 wrap)
11	Gold 4mm Silk	Straight
12	Yellow 4mm Silk	Lazy Daisy
13	Yellow 4mm Silk	Ribbon
14	729 floss (1 strand)	Pistil
15	Button	Beading

Optional Color Combination

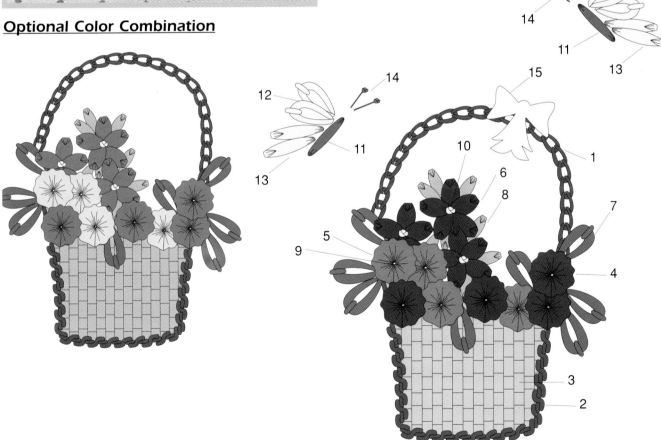

Pretty Pig

	Ribbon/DMC Floss	Stitch
1	Pink 4mm Silk	Whipped Running
2	Blue 4mm Silk	Loop
3	Blue 4mm Silk	Straight
4	Blue 4mm Silk	French Knot (1 wrap)
5	827 floss (1 strand)	Straight
6	Rose 4mm Silk	Straight
7	Pink 4mm Silk	Satin
8	Rose 4mm Silk	Whipped Running
9	White 4mm Silk	Lazy Daisy
10	Yellow 4mm Silk	French Knot (1 wrap)
11	Green 4mm Silk	Whipped Running
12	Green 4mm Silk	Lazy Daisy
13	Green 4mm Silk	Ribbon
14	Black 4mm Silk	French Knot (1 wrap)

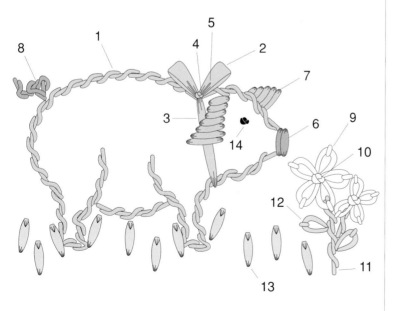

Clown

	Ribbon/DMC Floss	Stitch
1	White 4mm Silk	Satin
2	Red 4mm Silk	Satin
3	321 floss (1 strand)	Stem
4	321 floss (1 strand)	Straight
5	Black 4mm Silk	French Knot (1 wrap)
6	Black 4mm Silk	Straight
7	Red 4mm Silk	French Knot (2 wraps)
8	Red 4mm Silk	Backstitch
9	Dk. Peach 4mm Silk	Straight
10	White 7mm Silk	Loop
11	Gold Med. Braid	Couched

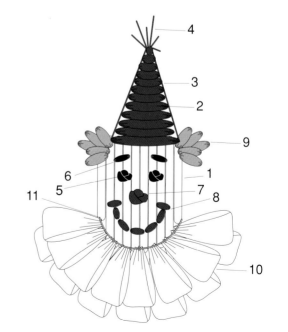

Balloon Bunch

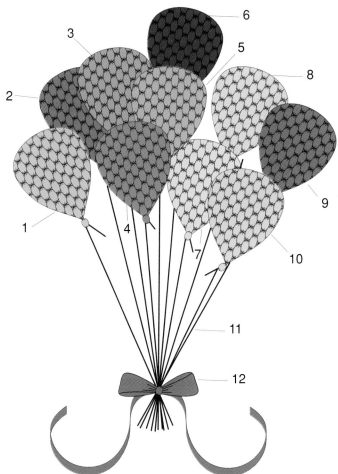

	Ribbon/DMC Floss	Stitch
1	Turquoise 4mm Silk	Long & Short
2	Orange 4mm Silk	Long & Short
3	Dk. Green 4mm Silk	Long & Short
4	Purple 4mm Silk	Long & Short
5	Coral 4mm Silk	Long & Short
6	Red 4mm Silk	Long & Short
7	Yellow 4mm Silk	Long & Short
8	Blue 4mm Silk	Long & Short
9	Magenta 4mm Silk	Long & Short
10	Lt. Green 4mm Silk	Long & Short
11	844 floss (2 strands)	Stem
12	Magenta 4mm Silk	Bow—Tacking

Additional Design

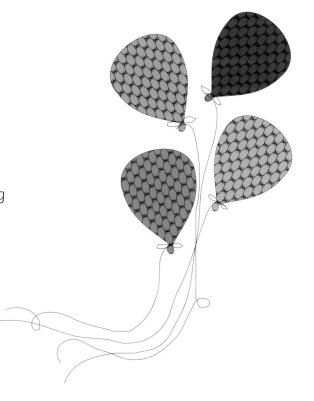

Sunny Flower

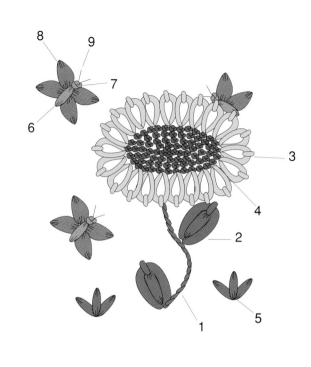

	Ribbon/DMC Floss	Stitch		Ribbon/DMC Floss	Stitch
1	Green 4mm Silk	Stem	**6**	Gray 4mm Silk	Straight
2	Green 4mm Silk	Decorative Lazy Daisy	**7**	Gray 4mm Silk	French Knot
3	Yellow 4mm Silk	Lazy Daisy			(1 wrap)
4	Brown 4mm Silk	French Knot	**8**	Orange 4mm Silk	Padded Straight
		(1 wrap)	**9**	310 floss (1 strand)	Straight
5	Green 4mm Silk	Straight			

Additional Design

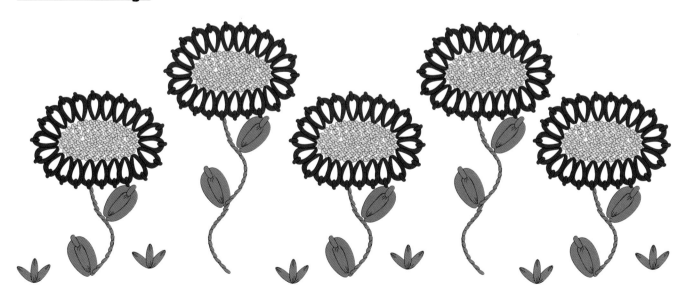

Grapes Sachet

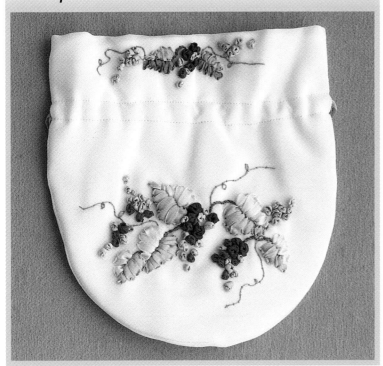

Ribbon/DMC Floss	Stitch
1 869 floss (2 strands)	Stem
2 3012 floss (1 strand)	Couched
3 Lt. Green 4mm Silk	Ribbon
4 Green 4mm Silk	Ribbon
5 Dk. Green 4mm Silk	Ribbon
6 Dk. Purple 4mm Silk	Colonial Knot
7 Med. Purple 4mm Silk	French Knot (1 wrap)
8 Lt. Purple 4mm Silk	Colonial Knot
9 Lavender 4mm Silk	French Knot (1 wrap)

Additional Designs

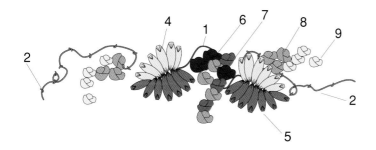

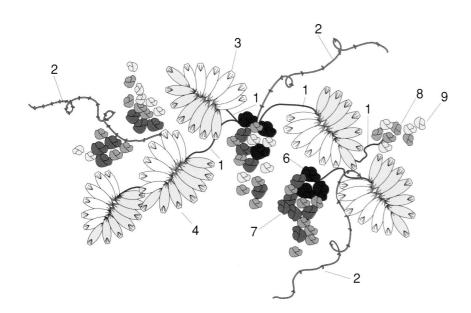

Angelfish

Ribbon/DMC Floss	Stitch
1 Orange 4mm Silk couched with 720 floss (1 strand)	Couched
2 White 4mm Silk	Ribbon
3 White 4mm Silk	Straight
4 Black 4mm Silk	French Knot (1 wrap)
5 720 floss (1 strand)	Stem
6 720 floss (1 strand)	French Knot (1 wrap)
7 Green 4mm Silk	Fly
8 501 floss (1 strand)	Stem

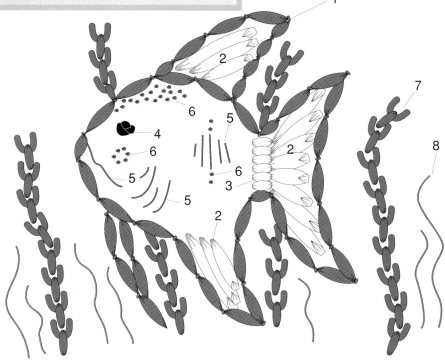

Additional Design

Picnic Basket

Ribbon/DMC Floss	Stitch
1 Gold 4mm Silk	Woven Ribbon
2 Gold 4mm Silk	Chain
3 Brown 4mm Silk	Stem
4 Rose 4mm Silk	Satin
5 Green 4mm Silk	Stem
6 Black 4mm Silk	French Knot (1 wrap)
7 White 4mm Silk	Stem
8 Black 4mm Silk	Straight
9 Black 4mm Silk	Padded Straight
10 310 floss (1 strand)	Straight

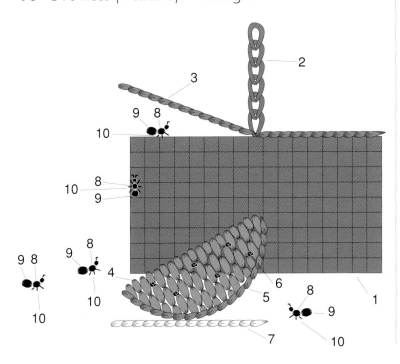

Fluttering Butterflies

Ribbon/DMC Floss	Stitch
1 Blue 4mm Silk	Straight
2 Orange 4mm Silk	Straight
3 Yellow 4mm Silk	Straight
4 Brown 4mm Silk	Whipped Running
5 310 floss (1 strand)	Stem
6 310 floss (1 strand)	French Knot (1 wrap)

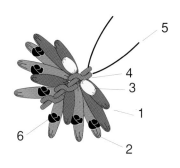

Love Grows Here

Ribbon/DMC Floss	Stitch
1 957 floss (2 strands)	Stem
2 Dk. Pink 4mm Silk	Woven Ribbon
3 Dk. Pink 4mm Silk	Outline
4 Dk. Green 4mm Silk	Stem
5 Dk. Green 4mm Silk	Lazy Daisy

Optional Verse

two hearts entwined forever

Wishing Well

	Ribbon/DMC Floss	Stitch
1	Brown 4mm Silk woven with Dk. Brown 4mm Silk	Woven Ribbon
2	Brown 4mm Silk tacked with 869 floss (1 strand)	Straight
3	Brown 4mm Silk	Whipped Running
4	Brown 4mm Silk tacked with 869 floss (1 strand)	Straight
5	Lt. Blue 4mm Silk	French Knot (1 wrap)
6	Med. Blue 4mm Silk	French Knot (1 wrap)
7	Rose 4mm Silk	French Knot (1 wrap)
8	Dk. Green 4mm Silk	Straight
9	902 floss (1 strand)	Stem

Optional Color Combination

Milk Can

Ribbon/DMC Floss	Stitch
1 Lt. Blue 4mm Silk	Whipped Running
2 Lt. Blue 4mm Silk	Straight
3 310 floss (1 strand)	Straight
4 310 floss (1 strand)	Stem
5 310 floss (1 strand)	French Knot (2 wraps)
6 3347 floss (2 strands)	Stem
7 Lt. Green 4mm Silk	Straight
8 Peach 4mm Silk	Loop
9 Coral 4mm Silk	Loop
10 445 floss (1 strand)	French Knot (3 wraps)

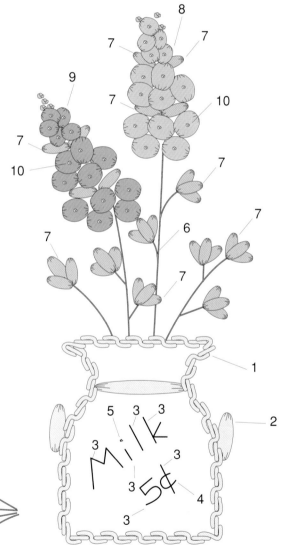

Additional Design

For Baby

Ribbon/DMC Floss	Stitch
1 Off-white 4mm Silk couched with 739 floss (1 strand)	Couched
2 Off-white 4mm Silk	Straight
3 Lt. Peach 4mm Silk	Lazy Daisy
4 Salmon 4mm Silk	Lazy Daisy
5 Lt. Green 4mm Silk	Straight
6 White Beads	Beading

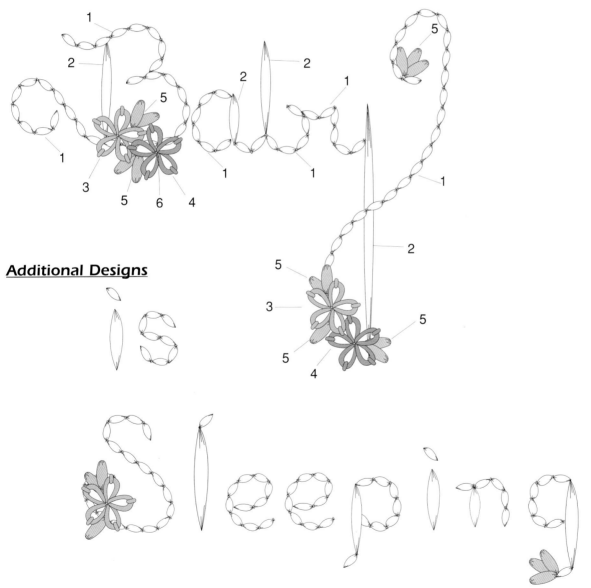

Additional Designs

ABC

	Ribbon/DMC Floss	Stitch
1	3078 floss (3 strands)	Chain
2	334 floss (3 strands)	Chain
3	3689 floss (3 strands)	Chain
4	Lt. Yellow 4mm Silk couched with 3078 floss (1 strand)	Couched
5	Med. Blue 4mm Silk couched with 334 floss (1 strand)	Couched
6	Lt. Pink 4mm Silk couched with 3689 floss (1 strand)	Couched
7	Lavender 4mm Silk	Straight
8	White 4mm Silk	French Knot (1 wrap)
9	Green 4mm Silk	Lazy Daisy

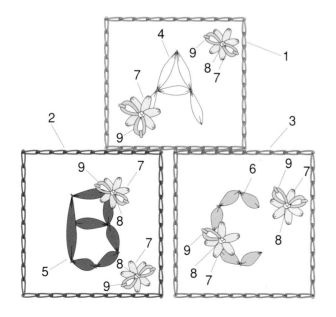

I Love You

	Ribbon/DMC Floss	Stitch
1	Rose 4mm Silk	Whipped Running (1 wrap)
2	Lt. Pink 4mm Silk	Spider Web Rose
3	Green 4mm Silk	Lazy Daisy
4	603 floss (1 strand) Silver Filament (1 strand)	Stem
5	603 floss (1 strand) Silver Filament (1 strand)	Straight
6	603 floss (2 strands)	Backstitch

Love & Flowers

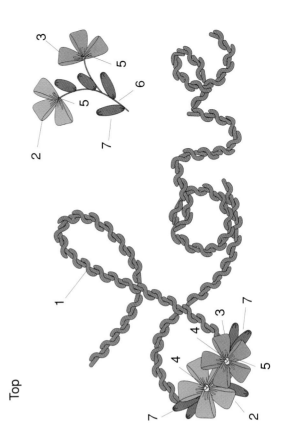

Top

Ribbon/DMC Floss	Stitch
1 Dusty Purple 4mm Silk	Whipped Running
2 Pink 4mm Silk	Loop
3 Purple 4mm Silk	Loop
4 739 floss (2 strands)	French Knot (5 wraps)
5 739 floss (2 strands)	Straight
6 3363 floss (3 strands)	Stem
7 Green 4mm Silk	Straight

Additional Design

Friendship is Love with Understanding

Be Mine

	Ribbon/DMC Floss	Stitch
1	3685 floss (2 strands)	Chain
2	3664 floss (1 strand)	Stem
3	Lavender 4mm Silk	Straight
4	Lavender 4mm Silk couched with 3609 floss (1 strand)	Couched
5	Lavender 4mm Silk	Pistil
6	Rose 4mm Silk	Spider Web Rose
7	Blue 4mm Silk	French Knot (1 wrap)

	Ribbon/DMC Floss	Stitch
8	Yellow 4mm Silk	French Knot (1 wrap)
9	Violet 4mm Silk	Ribbon
10	3078 floss (1 strand)	French Knot (3 wraps)
11	3078 floss (1 strand)	Pistil
12	Lt. Blue Beads	Beading
13	Green 4mm Silk	Lazy Daisy
14	3722 floss (1 strand)	Stem

Additional Designs

To Have and To Hold

Ribbon/DMC Floss	Stitch
1 Dusty Purple 4mm Silk couched with 3041 floss (1 strand)	Couched
2 3364 floss (1 strand)	Chain
3 Purple 4mm Silk	Lazy Daisy
4 Rose 4mm Silk	Lazy Daisy
5 Green 4mm Silk	Straight
6 Dusty Purple 4mm Silk	French Knot (1 wrap)

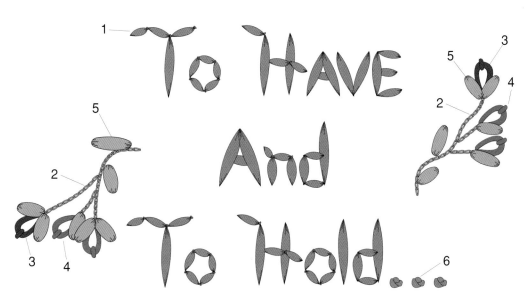

Additional Designs

A Bouquet for You

Ribbon/DMC Floss   Stitch

1   561 floss (2 strands)   Stem

2   Lt. Green 4mm Silk   Decorative Lazy Daisy
     with Dk. Green 4mm Silk center

3   Dk. Green 4mm   Decorative Lazy Daisy
     with Lt. Green 4mm Silk center

4   Dk. Green 4mm Silk   Straight

5   Lt. Green 4mm Silk   Straight

6   Burgundy 4mm Silk   Padded Straight Bud
     with Dk. Green 4mm Silk leaves

7   Pink 4mm Silk   Padded Straight Bud
     with Dk. Green 4mm Silk leaves

8   Yellow 4mm Silk   Padded Straight Bud
     with Lt. Green 4mm Silk leaves

9   Yellow 4mm Silk   Spider Web Rose

10   Pink 4mm Silk   Spider Web Rose

11   Rose 4mm Silk   Spider Web Rose
     Burgundy 4mm Silk

12   3608 floss (4 strands)   French Knot
     (2 wraps)

13   327 floss (6 strands)   French Knot
     (2 wraps)

14   327 floss (2 strands)   Backstitch

Additional Designs

Friends Forever

	Ribbon/DMC Floss	Stitch
1	2621 floss (2 strands)	Stem
2	Dk. Green 4mm Silk with Lt. Green 4mm Silk center	Decorative Lazy Daisy
3	Lt. Green 4mm with Dk. Green 4mm Silk center	Decorative Lazy Daisy
4	Lt. Green 4mm Silk	Straight
5	Dk. Green 4mm Silk	Straight
6	Red 4mm Silk with Lt. Green 4mm Silk leaves	Padded Straight Bud
7	White 4mm Silk with Dk. Green 4mm Silk leaves	Padded Straight Bud
8	Pink 4mm Silk with Lt. Green 4mm Silk leaves	Padded Straight Bud
9	Pink 4mm Silk	Spider Web Rose
10	White 4mm Silk	Spider Web Rose
11	Red 4mm Silk	Spider Web Rose
12	3676 floss (4 strands)	French Knot (2 wraps)
13	2650 floss (6 strands)	French Knot (2 wraps)
14	2621 floss (2 strands)	Backstitch

Additional Designs

Love In Bloom

	Ribbon/DMC Floss	Stitch
1	3364 floss (2 strands)	Chain
2	3364 floss (2 strands)	Stem
3	Off-white 4mm Silk	Stem Rose
4	Off-white 4mm Silk	Decorative Lazy Daisy
5	Dusty Purple 4mm Silk	French Knot (2 wraps)
6	Dk. Purple 4mm Silk	French Knot (2 wraps)
7	Green 4mm Silk	Lazy Daisy
8	Green 4mm Silk	Straight
9	319 floss (1 strand)	Stem

Additional Design

Easter Wishes

	Ribbon/DMC Floss	Stitch		Ribbon/DMC Floss	Stitch
1	Lt. Green 4mm Silk woven with Yellow 4mm Silk	Woven Ribbon	**4**	Lt. Pink 4mm Silk	Satin
			5	Rose 4mm Silk	Loop
			6	Rose 4mm Silk	Straight
2	Yellow 4mm Silk	Whipped Running	**7**	3347 floss (1 strand)	Straight
3	Lt. Blue 4mm Silk	Satin	**8**	959 floss (2 strands)	Stem

Optional Color Combination

	Ribbon/DMC Floss	Stitch			Ribbon/DMC Floss	Stitch
1	503 floss (1 strand)	Chain		**6**	Lt. Yellow 4mm Silk	French Knot
2	Lavender 4mm Silk	French Knot				(1 wrap)
		(1 wrap)		**7**	Lt. Pink 4mm Silk	Satin
3	Dk. Pink 4mm Silk	Ribbon		**8**	605 floss (1 strand)	Stem
4	Lt. Pink 4mm Silk	Ribbon		**9**	605 floss (1 strand)	Straight
5	Lt. Blue 4mm Silk	French Knot		**10**	Green 4mm Silk	Lazy Daisy
		(1 wrap)		**11**	333 floss (1 strand)	Stem

Additional Design

Father's Day

	Ribbon/DMC Floss	Stitch
1	Dk. Green 4mm Silk	Satin
2	Gold 4mm Silk	Straight
3	White 4mm Silk	Straight
4	Brown 4mm Silk	Stem
5	Dk. Gray 4mm Silk	Stem
6	White 4mm Silk	Lazy Daisy
7	Lt. Gray 4mm Silk	Lazy Daisy
8	Black 4mm Silk	Stem
9	Lt. Gray 4mm Silk	Straight
10	Dk. Gray 4mm Silk	Straight
11	Brown 4mm Silk	French Knot (2 wraps)
12	Med. Blue 4mm Silk couched with 322 floss (1 strand)	Couched
13	Black 4mm Silk	Straight

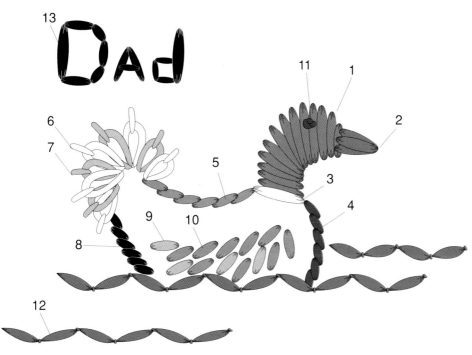

Optional Color Combinations

Packages

Ribbon/DMC Floss	Stitch
1 Green 4mm Silk	Woven Ribbon
2 Red 4mm Silk	Woven Ribbon
3 Gold 4mm Silk	Woven Ribbon
4 Red 4mm Silk	Straight
5 Blue 4mm Silk	Straight
6 Gold 4mm Silk	Straight
7 Red 4mm Silk	Loop
8 Blue 4mm Silk	Loop
9 Gold 4mm Silk	Loop

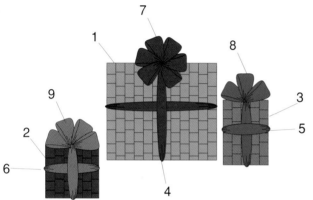

Optional Color Combination

Additional Designs

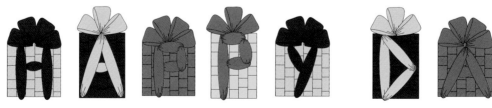

Spring Heart Wreath

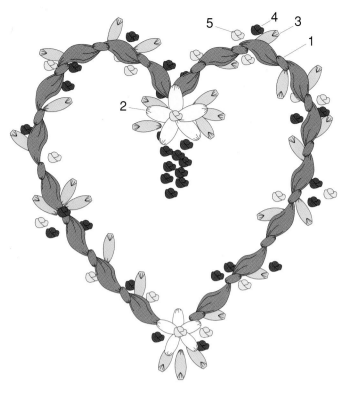

Ribbon/DMC Floss	Stitch		Ribbon/DMC Floss	Stitch
1 Pink 7mm Organdy	Whipped Running	4	Purple 4mm Silk	French Knot (1 wrap)
2 Cream 7mm Silk	Straight	5	Off-white 4mm Silk	French Knot (1 wrap)
3 Lt. Green 4mm Silk	Ribbon			

Dove

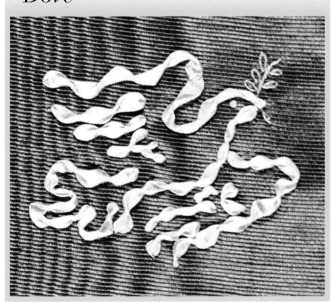

Ribbon/DMC Floss	Stitch
1 White 4mm Silk couched with White floss (1 strand)	Couched
2 White 4mm Silk	French Knot (1 wrap)
3 739 floss (1 strand)	Stem
4 739 floss (1 strand)	Lazy Daisy

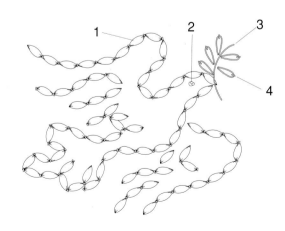

Boo!

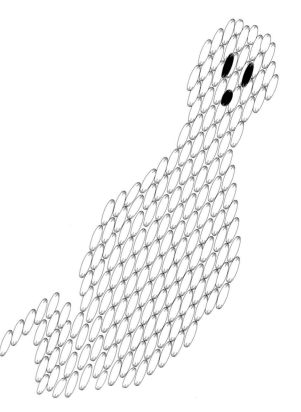

	Ribbon/DMC Floss	Stitch
1	Orange 4mm Silk	Long & Short
2	White 7mm Silk	Long & Short
3	Black 4mm Silk	Straight
4	Black 4mm Silk	Backstitch
5	Dk. Green 4mm Silk	Satin

	Ribbon/DMC Floss	Stitch
6	Orange 4mm Silk	Whipped Running
7	Orange 4mm Silk	Straight
8	Orange 4mm Silk	French Knot
		(2 wraps)

Additional Designs

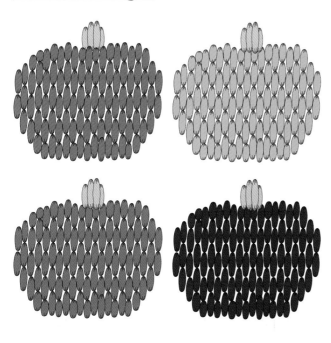

Happy Haunting

	Ribbon/DMC Floss	Stitch
1	Dk. Gray 4mm Silk	Chain
2	Dk. Gray 4mm Silk	Satin
3	Black 4mm Silk	Backstitch
4	310 floss (1 strand)	Backstitch
5	647 floss (2 strands)	Backstitch
6	Black 4mm Silk	French Knot (1 wrap)
7	310 floss (1 strand)	French Knot (3 wraps)
8	310 floss (1 strand)	Straight
9	Brown 4mm Silk couched with 435 floss (1 strand)	Couched
10	White 4mm Silk	Long & Short
11	Black 4mm Silk	Straight
12	Black 4mm Silk	French Knot (1 wrap)
13	435 floss (2 strands)	Straight
14	310 floss (1 strand)	Straight
15	Silver Med. Braid	Chain
16	Silver Med. Braid	Stem

Additional Design

Candy Cane

Ribbon/DMC Floss — Stitch

	Ribbon/DMC Floss	Stitch
1	Red 7mm Silk	Straight
2	White 7mm Silk	Straight

Additional Design

Happy Holidays

Holly & Candy Canes

Ribbon/DMC Floss — Stitch

	Ribbon/DMC Floss	Stitch
1	Red 7mm Silk White 7mm Silk	Whipped Running
2	Dk. Green 4mm Silk	Ribbon
3	Red 7mm Silk	French Knot (2 wraps)

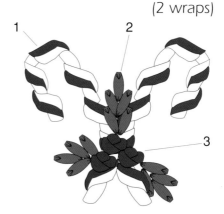

Optional Color Combination

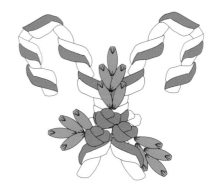

Hurricane Candle

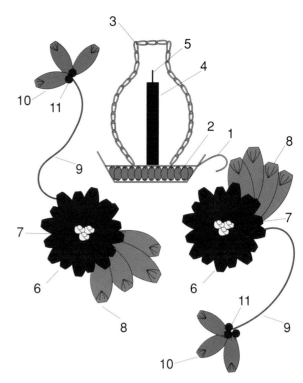

	Ribbon/DMC Floss	Stitch
1	435 floss (1 strand)	Stem
	Gold Filament (1 strand)	
2	Gold 4mm Silk	Satin
3	739 floss (1 strand)	Chain
4	321 floss (2 strands)	Satin
5	310 floss (1 strand)	Straight
6	Red 4mm Silk	Ribbon

	Ribbon/DMC Floss	Stitch
7	Yellow 4mm Silk	French Knot
		(2 wraps)
8	Green 4mm Silk	Ribbon
9	3345 floss (2 strands)	Stem
10	Green 4mm Silk	Ribbon
11	Red Beads	Beading

Additional Designs

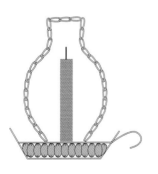

Candle Heart

Ribbon/DMC Floss		Stitch
3	Lt. Yellow 7mm Silk	Ribbon
4	Lt. Yellow 7mm Silk	Straight
5	Bright Yellow 4mm Silk	Ribbon
6	Dk. Green 7mm Silk	Ribbon
7	319 floss (3 strands)	Straight
8	Red 4mm Silk	French Knot (1 wrap)
9	White 4mm Silk	Ribbon
10	Red 4mm Silk	Ribbon
11	Bright Yellow 4mm Silk	French Knot (1 wrap)
12	Dk. Green 4mm Silk	Lazy Daisy
13	Lt. Green 4mm Silk	Lazy Daisy
14	Red 7mm Silk / White 7mm Silk	Loop
15	Red 7mm Silk / White 7mm Silk	Tacked Ribbon
16	Gold Med. Braid	Straight

Ribbon/DMC Floss		Stitch
1	Red 7mm Silk	Tacked Ribbon
2	White 4mm Silk	French Knot (2 wraps)

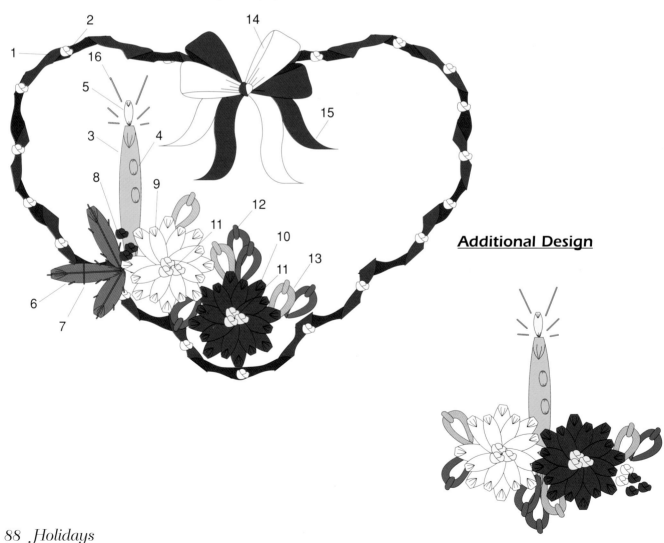

Additional Design

Candle Centerpiece

Ribbon/DMC Floss

	Ribbon/DMC Floss	Stitch
1	Red 4mm Silk	Whipped Running
2	Yellow 4mm Silk	Straight
3	729 floss (2 strands)	Straight
4	310 floss (1 strand)	Straight
5	Green 4mm Silk	Straight
6	Dk. Red 4mm Silk	French Knot (1 wrap)

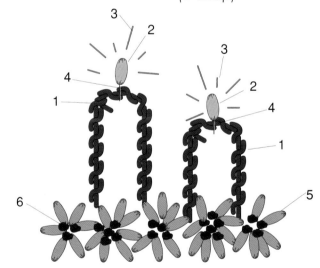

Additional Design

Three Candles

	Ribbon/DMC Floss	Stitch
1	Yellow 4mm Silk	Whipped Running
2	310 floss (1 strand)	Straight
3	Yellow 4mm Silk	Straight
4	729 floss (1 strand)	Straight
5	Green 4mm Silk	Straight
6	Red Beads	Beading

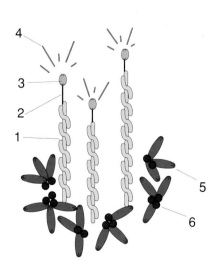

Festive Wreath

	Ribbon/DMC Floss	Stitch
1	Green 7mm Silk	Ribbon
2	Lt. Green 4mm Silk	Ribbon
3	Red 4mm Silk	French Knot (3 wraps)
4	Gold 4mm Silk	Pinecone
5	White Beads	Beading
6	Red 7mm Silk couched with 321 floss (1 strand)	Couched

Red Bow Wreath

	Ribbon/DMC Floss	Stitch
1	Green 4mm Silk	Lazy Daisy
2	Brown 4mm Silk	Bullion
3	Gold Med. Braid	Threading
4	Red 4mm Silk	Bow—Tacking
5	Bell	Beading
6	Red Beads	Beading

Holly Garland

Ribbon/DMC Floss	Stitch
1 Silver Med. Braid couched with Gold Fine Braid	Couched
2 Dk. Green 4mm Silk	Ribbon
3 3345 floss (1 strand)	Straight
4 Red 4mm Silk	Loop

Ribbon/DMC Floss	Stitch
5 Red 4mm Silk	Straight
6 Red 4mm Silk	French Knot (1 wrap)
7 321 floss (1 strand)	Straight
8 Red Beads	Beading

Joy

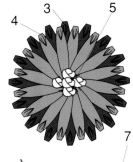

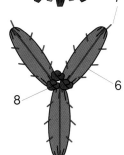

Ribbon/DMC Floss	Stitch
1 Red 4mm Silk	Straight
2 White 4mm Silk	Straight
3 Red 4mm Silk	Ribbon
4 Pink 4mm Silk	Ribbon
5 Yellow 4mm Silk	French Knot (2 wraps)
6 Dk. Green 4mm Silk	Straight
7 3345 floss (1 strand)	Straight
8 Red 4mm Silk	French Knot (1 wrap)

Optional Color Combinations

Joy to the World

Ribbon/DMC Floss	Stitch
1 White 4mm Silk couched with White floss (1 strand)	Couched
2 White 4mm Silk	Straight
3 Green 4mm Silk	Ribbon
4 Red 4mm Silk	French Knot (1 wrap)

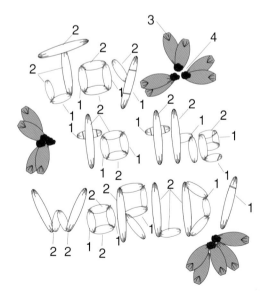

Ho Ho Ho

Ribbon/DMC Floss	Stitch
1 Red 4mm Silk	Whipped Running
2 White 4mm Silk	Ribbon
3 729 floss (1 strand)	French Knot (3 wraps)
4 Lt. Green 4mm Silk	Lazy Daisy
5 Dk. Green 4mm Silk	Straight
6 Lt. Green 4mm Silk	Straight
7 Red Beads	Beading

Taper Candles

Ribbon/DMC Floss	Stitch		Ribbon/DMC Floss	Stitch
1 Red 4mm Silk	Stem	**4**	Red 4mm Silk	French Knot (1 wrap)
2 Yellow 4mm Silk	Lazy Daisy			
3 Dk. Green 4mm Silk	Leaf	**5**	Brown 4mm Silk	Straight

Additional Design

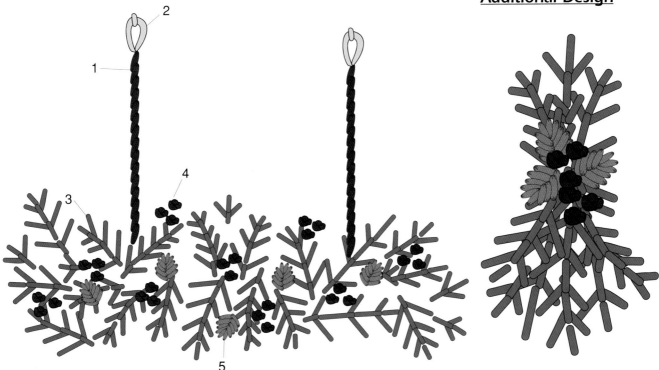

	Ribbon/DMC Floss	Stitch		Ribbon/DMC Floss	Stitch
1	Green 4mm Silk couched with 319 floss (1 strand)	Couched	**8**	Red 7mm Silk	French Knot (3 wraps)
2	Red 7mm Silk	Lazy Daisy	**9**	Gold 4mm Silk	Pinecone
3	Red 4mm Silk	Lazy Daisy	**10**	White 7mm Silk	Folded Rose
4	Dk. Green 7mm Silk	Ribbon	**11**	Red 4mm Silk	French Knot (1 wrap)
5	Green 4mm Silk	Ribbon			
6	Dk. Green 7mm Silk	Straight	**12**	Gold Fine Braid	Stem
7	319 floss (1 strand)	Straight	**13**	Green Bead	Beading
			14	Gold Bead	Beading

Reindeer

Ribbon/DMC Floss	Stitch
1	Twig—Tacked
2 Brown 4mm Silk	Open Lazy Daisy
3 Brown 4mm Silk couched with 435 floss (1 strand)	Couched
4 Black 4mm Silk	Couched
5 Black 4mm Silk	French Knot (1 wrap)

Ribbon/DMC Floss	Stitch
6 Dk. Red 4mm Silk	French Knot (3 wraps)
7 Green 4mm Silk	Ribbon
8 Red 4mm Silk	French Knot (1 wrap)
9 Green Fine Braid	Threading

Additional Designs

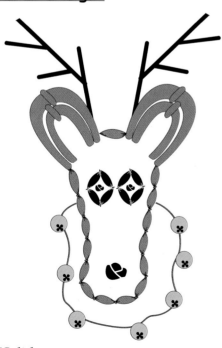

Rudolph

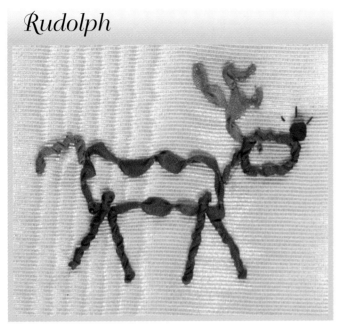

Ribbon/DMC Floss	Stitch
1 Brown 4mm Silk couched with 782 floss (1 strand)	Couched
2 Brown 4mm Silk	Whipped Running (1 wrap)
3 Gold 4mm Silk	Whipped Running
4 Gold 4mm Silk couched with 782 floss (1 strand)	Couched
5 Red 4mm Silk	French Knot (2 wraps)
6 782 floss (1 strand)	French Knot (2 wraps)
7 349 floss (1 strand)	Straight

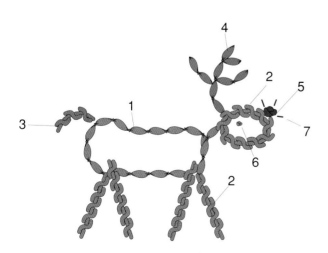

Santa's Helper

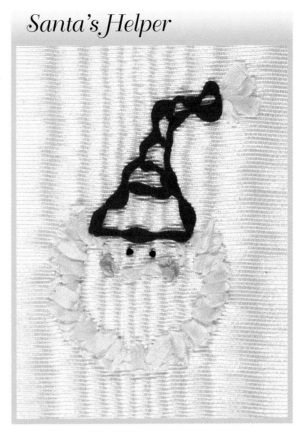

Ribbon/DMC Floss	Stitch
1 White 4mm Silk	Ribbon
2 White 4mm Silk couched with White floss (1 strand)	Couched
3 Pink 4mm Silk	Ribbon
4 Red 4mm Silk couched with 666 floss (1 strand)	Couched
5 White 4mm Silk	Ribbon
6 310 floss (1 strand)	French Knot (3 wraps)

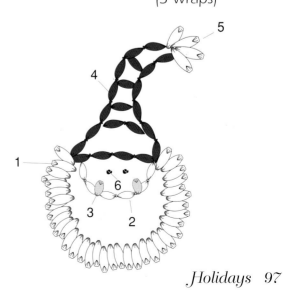

Santa Claus

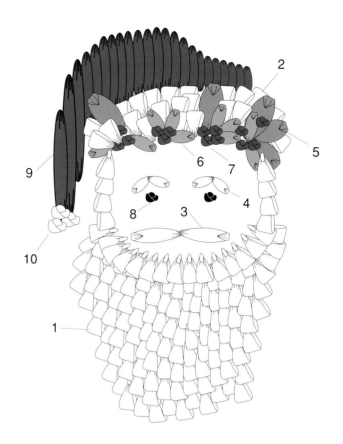

	Ribbon/DMC Floss	Stitch
1	White 4mm Silk	Plume
2	White 4mm Silk	Plume
3	White 4mm Silk	Ribbon
4	White 4mm Silk	Ribbon
5	Lt. Green 7mm Silk	Ribbon
6	Green 4mm Silk	Ribbon
7	Red 4mm Silk	French Knot (1 wrap)

	Ribbon/DMC Floss	Stitch
8	Black 4mm Silk	French Knot (1 wrap)
9	Red 4mm Silk	Satin
10	White 4mm Silk	French Knot (3 wraps)

Additional Design

The minds of children muse to know the mystery that is Santa.

The hearts of children yearn to feel the love and joy that are Christmas.

Berry Wreath

Ribbon/DMC Floss   Stitch

1 Gold 4mm Silk   Whipped Running
whipped with Rust 4mm Silk
and Gold Fine Braid

2 Dk. Green 4mm Silk   Lazy Daisy

3 Lt. Green 4mm Silk   Straight

4 Rust 4mm Silk   Pinecone
Gold 4mm Silk

5 Red 4mm Silk   French Knot (1 wrap)

Ribbon/DMC Floss   Stitch

6 Red 4mm Silk   Bow—Tacking
Gold 4mm Silk
Rust 4mm Silk

Optional Color Combination & Additional Designs

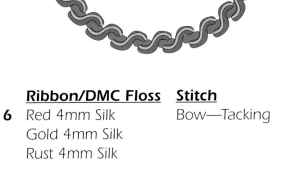

	Ribbon/DMC Floss	Stitch		Ribbon/DMC Floss	Stitch
1	Brown 4mm Silk	Chain	**9**	782 floss (1 strand)	Straight
2	782 floss (2 strands)	Chain	**10**	Green 4mm Silk	Ribbon
3	Dk. Red 4mm Silk	Ribbon	**11**	Red 4mm Silk	Whipped Running
4	Peach 4mm Silk	Ribbon	**12**	White 4mm Silk	Padded Straight
5	725 floss (1 strand)	French Knot (3 wraps)	**13**	Red Beads	Beading
6	725 floss (3 strands)	Stem	**14**	919 floss (1 strand)	Chain
7	310 floss (3 strands)	Straight	**15**	Red 4mm Silk	Straight
8	Yellow 4mm Silk	Straight	**16**	Button	Beading

9

8

7

6

10

4

3

5

2

16

13

10

10

13

1

15

14

15

14

12

12

11

11

10

13

10

13

Additional Designs

Holidays 101

Sled

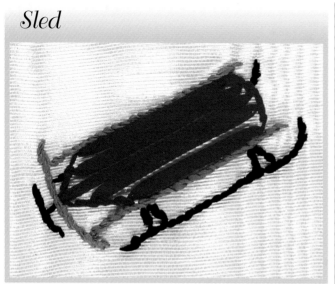

Ribbon/DMC Floss	Stitch
1 Black 4mm Silk	Stem
2 Gold 4mm Silk	Stem
3 Red 4mm Silk	Stem
4 Red 4mm Silk	Straight

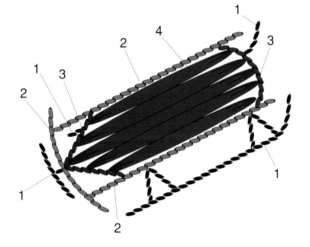

Additional Design

Sleigh

Ribbon/DMC Floss	Stitch
1 Gold 4mm Silk	Whipped Running
2 435 floss (1 strand) Gold Fine Braid	Stem
3 Red 4mm Silk tacked with 666 floss (1 strand)	Lazy Daisy
4 Off-white 4mm Silk tacked with Ecru floss (1 strand)	Lazy Daisy
5 Dk. Green 4mm Silk	Lazy Daisy
6 Dk. Green 4mm Silk	Straight
7 727 floss (1 strand)	French Knot (5 wraps)
8 Red 4mm Silk	French Knot (1 wrap)
9 Green Med. Braid	Straight
10 Gold 4mm Silk	French Knot (2 wraps)

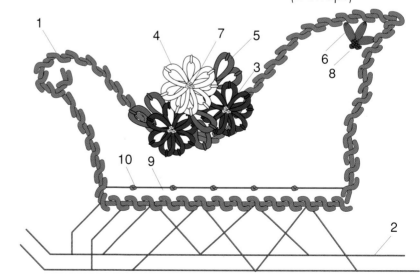

Snowman

	Ribbon/DMC Floss	Stitch
1	White 4mm Silk	Whipped Running
2	White 4mm Silk	Woven Ribbon
3	Black 4mm Silk	Straight
4	Brown 4mm Silk	Straight
5	310 floss (2 strands)	French Knot (3 wraps)
6	310 floss (1 strand)	Straight
7	970 floss (3 strands)	Padded Straight
8	Yellow 4mm Silk	Straight
9	Gold Med. Braid	Straight
10	Red 4mm Silk tacked with 321 floss (1 strand)	Tacked Ribbon

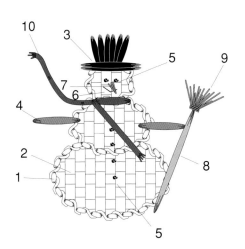

Poinsettia Stocking

	Ribbon/DMC Floss	Stitch
1	Red 4mm Silk	Ribbon
2	Lt. Green 4mm Silk	Straight
3	Dk. Green 4mm Silk	Straight
4	Yellow 4mm Silk	French Knot (1 wrap)

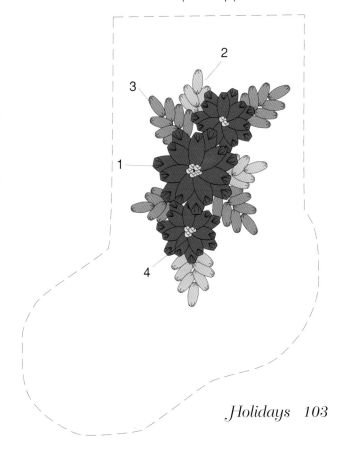

Three Bells

	Ribbon/DMC Floss	Stitch
1	Gold 4mm Silk	Stem
2	Gold 4mm Silk	French Knot (2 wraps)
3	Dk. Green 4mm Silk	Ribbon
4	Red 4mm Silk	French Knot (1 wrap)

Optional Color Combination

Christmas Bells

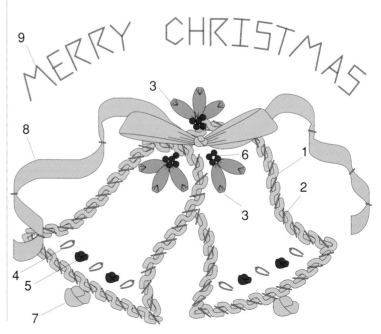

	Ribbon/DMC Floss	Stitch
1	Lt. Gray 4mm Silk	Whipped Running
2	Green Med. Braid Gold Fine Braid	Whipping
3	Green 4mm Silk	Ribbon
4	989 floss (2 strands)	Lazy Daisy
5	Red 4mm Silk	French Knot (1 wrap)
6	Red Bead	Beading
7	Yellow 4mm Silk	French Knot (1 wrap)
8	Yellow 4mm Silk couched with 729 floss (1 strand)	Bow—Tacking
9	Green Med. Braid	Backstitch

Simple Tree

Ribbon/DMC Floss	Stitch
1 Green 4mm Silk tacked with 890 floss (1 strand)	Tacked Ribbon
2 Red 4mm Silk	French Knot (2 wraps)

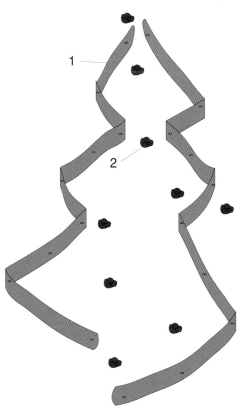

Icicle Tree

Ribbon/DMC Floss	Stitch
1 Dk. Green 4mm Silk couched with 3345 floss (1 strand)	Couched
2 Brown 4mm Silk	Straight
3 Red 4mm Silk	French Knot (2 wraps)
4 Silver Fine Braid	Straight
5 Gold Med. Braid	Straight

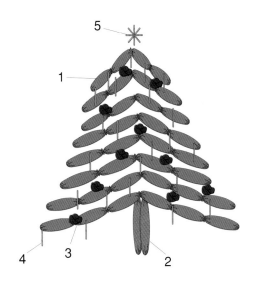

Tree Star

Ribbon/DMC Floss · Stitch

	Ribbon/DMC Floss	Stitch
1	Dk. Green 4mm Silk tacked with 890 floss (1 strand)	Tacked Ribbon
2	Red 4mm Silk	French Knot (2 wraps)
3	Yellow 4mm Silk	Straight

Express

Ribbon/DMC Floss · Stitch

	Ribbon/DMC Floss	Stitch
1	Brown 4mm Silk	Whipped Running
2	310 floss (1 strand)	Chain
3	Brown 4mm Silk	Straight
4	Black 4mm Silk	Whipped Running
5	310 floss (1 strand)	Straight
6	Dk. Green 4mm Silk	Leaf
7	Brown 4mm Silk	Straight
8	Lt. Green 4mm Silk	Straight
9	Red 4mm Silk	French Knot (1 wrap)
10	Gold Med. Braid	Couched
11	Gray 7mm Silk	French Knot (1 wrap)
12	321 floss (1 strand)	Backstitch

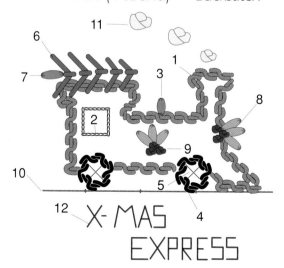

Santa Moon

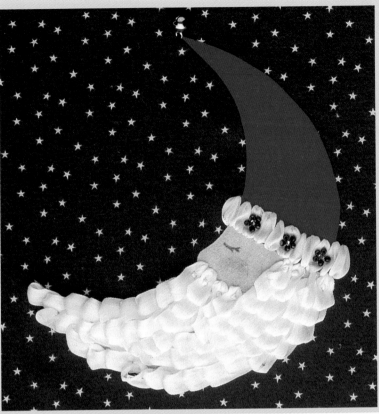

Fabric/Ribbon	Method/ Stitch
1 Red Cotton Fabric	Appliqué
2 Peach Cotton Fabric	Appliqué
3 White 7mm Silk	Plume
4 White 7mm Silk	Satin
5 Gold Beads	Beading
6 Green Beads	Beading
7 Bell	Beading
8 Face	Painting on Fabric

Additional Designs

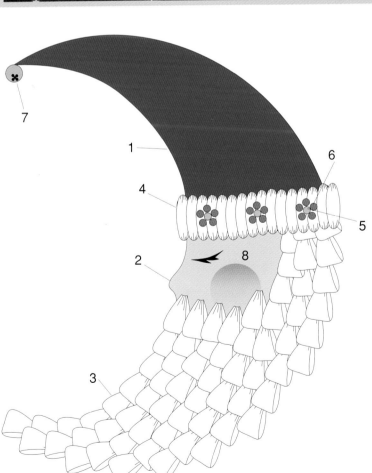

Santa Wreath

Fabric/Ribbon

1 Red Cotton Fabric
2 Peach Cotton Fabric
3 White 7mm Silk
4 Green 4mm Silk
5 Gold Fine Braid
6 Red Beads
7 Face

Method/Stitch

Appliqué
Appliqué
Plume
Lazy Daisy
Stem
Beading
Painting
on Fabric

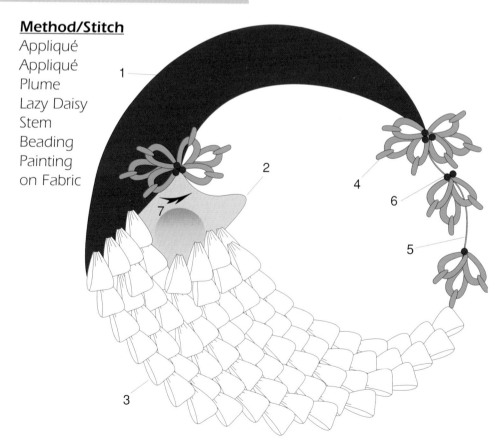

Acorn Wreath

Fabric/Ribbon/DMC Floss	Method/Stitch
1 Green Cotton Fabric	Appliqué
2 Tan Cotton Fabric	Appliqué
3 Brown Cotton Fabric	Appliqué
4 Yellow 4mm Silk	Ribbon
5 Orange 4mm Silk	Ribbon
6 Gold 4mm Silk	French Knot (3 wraps)
7 955 floss (1 strand)	Stem

	Fabric/Ribbon	**Method/ Stitch**		**Ribbon/DMC Floss**	**Method/ Stitch**
1	Med. Blue Cotton Fabric	Appliqué	**13**	Orange 7mm Silk	Couched
2	Brown Polished Apple Fabric	Appliqué	**14**	Dk. Green 4mm Silk	Straight
3	Brown and White Calico Fabric	Appliqué	**15**	469 floss (1 strand)	Stem
4	Tan and White Polk-a-dot Fabric	Appliqué	**16**	Yellow 4mm Silk	Couched
5	Tan and White Stripe Fabric	Appliqué	**17**	Bright Green 4mm Silk	Ribbon
6	Green Calico Fabric	Appliqué	**18**	Black 4mm Silk	Straight
7	Black Polished Apple Fabric	Appliqué	**19**	Brown 4mm Silk	Straight
8	Off-white Cotton Fabric	Appliqué	**20**	Red 4mm Silk	French Knot (1 wrap)
9	Red Cotton Fabric	Appliqué			
10	Brown Polished Apple Fabric	Appliqué	**21**	Ecru floss (2 strands)	Stem
11	Orange 7mm Silk	Satin	**22**	Off-white 4mm Silk	Ribbon
12	Lt. Green 4mm Silk	Straight	**23**	Off-white 4mm Silk	Chain

Top

Scarecrow

	Fabric/Ribbon/DMC Floss	Method/Stitch
1	Brown 4mm Silk	Whipped Running
2	Brown 4mm Silk	Couched
	couched with	
	420 floss (1 strand)	
3	Red and White Cotton Fabric	Appliqué
4	Red Bandanna Cotton Fabric	Appliqué
5	Lt. Yellow 4mm Silk	Straight
6	Blue Denim Cotton Fabric	Appliqué
7	Bright Yellow 4mm Silk	Whipped Running
8	Lt. Yellow 4mm Silk	Satin
9	Lt. Yellow 4mm Silk	Tacking
10	420 floss (2 strands)	Satin
11	Brown 4mm Silk	Chain

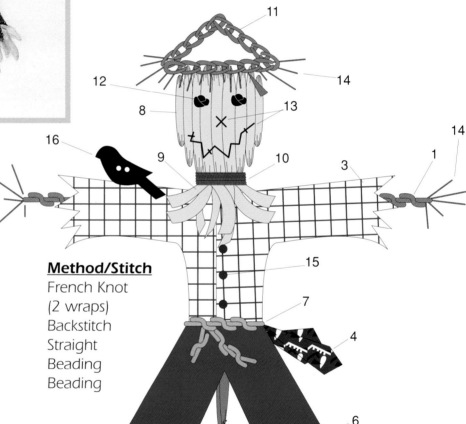

	Ribbon/DMC Floss	Method/Stitch
12	Black 4mm Silk	French Knot (2 wraps)
13	310 floss (2 strands)	Backstitch
14	420 floss (2 strands)	Straight
15	Red Beads	Beading
16	Button	Beading

Santa's Bag

Fabric/Ribbon/DMC Floss — Method/Stitch

	Fabric/Ribbon/DMC Floss	Method/Stitch
1	Pink and White Stripe Fabric	Appliqué
2	Pink Cotton Fabric	Appliqué
3	Peach Cotton Fabric	Appliqué
4	White Cotton Fabric	Appliqué
5	Tan Cotton Fabric	Appliqué
6	Brown Polished Apple Fabric	Appliqué
7	White Cotton Fabric	Appliqué
8	Brown 4mm Silk	Satin
9	420 floss (1 strand)	Straight

Enlarge 120 %.

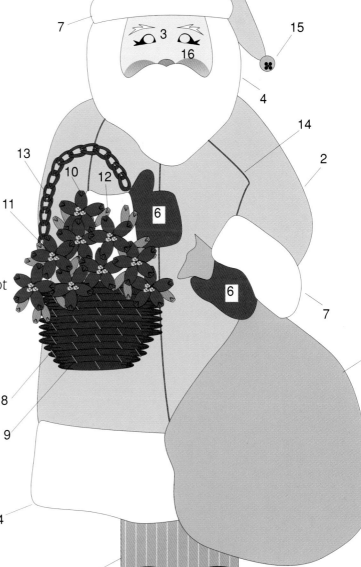

Ribbon/DMC Floss — Method/Stitch

	Ribbon/DMC Floss	Method/Stitch
10	Red 4mm Silk	Ribbon
11	745 floss (2 strands)	French Knot (3 wraps)
12	Green 4mm Silk	Ribbon
13	Brown 4mm Silk	Chain
14	3731 floss (1 strand)	Stem
15	Bell	Beading
16	Face	Painting on Fabric

Additional Design

Santa's Spruce

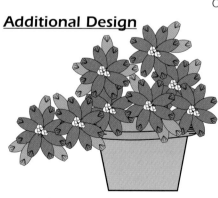

	Fabric/Ribbon/DMC Floss	Method/Stitch
1	Black Polished Apple Fabric	Appliqué
2	Pink and White Stripe Fabric	Appliqué
3	Pink Cotton Fabric	Appliqué
4	Black Polished Apple Fabric	Appliqué
5	Peach Cotton Fabric	Appliqué
6	White Cotton Fabric	Appliqué
7	Tan Cotton Fabric	Appliqué
8	Tan 4mm Silk	Straight

Enlarge 110%.

	Ribbon/DMC Floss	Method/Stitch
9	Red 4mm Silk	Ribbon
10	745 floss (2 strands)	French Knot (3 wraps)
11	Lt. Green 4mm Silk	Ribbon
12	Dk. Green 4mm Silk	Satin
13	Face	Painting on Fabric

Additional Design

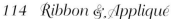

Spring Angel

Fabric/Ribbon/DMC Floss	Method/Stitch
1 Pink Cotton Fabric	Appliqué
2 White Cotton Fabric	Appliqué
3 Tan Cotton Fabric	Appliqué
4 Off-white Gathered Lace	Appliqué
5 Off-white Calico Fabric	Appliqué
6 Lt. Green Polk-a-dot Fabric	Appliqué
7 White Cotton Fabric	Appliqué
8 Peach Cotton Fabric	Appliqué
9 Pink Cotton Fabric	Appliqué
10 Lt. Green Polk-a-dot Fabric	Appliqué

Enlarge 115 %.

Ribbon/DMC Floss	Method/Stitch
11 Brown 4mm Silk	French Knot (3 wraps)
12 Coral 4mm Silk	Spider Web Rose
13 Coral 4mm Silk	French Knot (3 wraps)
14 Dk. Green 4mm Silk	Ribbon Chain
15 Yellow 4mm Silk	Bow— Tacking
16 Coral 4mm Silk	Painting on Fabric
17 Face	

Additional Design

Violets Angel

Fabric/Ribbon/DMC Floss	Method/Stitch
1 Off-white Calico Fabric	Appliqué
2 White Cotton Fabric	Appliqué
3 Brown Polished Apple Fabric	Appliqué
4 Lavender Cotton Fabric	Appliqué
5 White Cotton Eyelet Fabric	Appliqué
6 Peach Cotton Fabric	Appliqué
7 Lavender Cotton Fabric	Appliqué
8 Meran 28 ct. Fabric	Appliqué
9 White 4mm Silk	Straight
10 Brown 4mm Silk	Stem
11 Purple 4mm Silk	French Knot (1 wrap)
12 Lt. Purple 4mm Silk	French Knot (1 wrap)
13 Green 4mm Silk	Ribbon
14 Brown 4mm Silk	Straight
15 Lt. Brown 4mm Silk	Whipped Straight
16 Yellow 4mm Silk	Split
17 Face	Painting on Fabric

Enlarge 110 %.

Additional Design

Apple Basket Angel

Fabric/Ribbon/DMC Floss	Method/Stitch
1 Red Cotton Fabric	Appliqué
2 White Cotton Fabric	Appliqué
3 Brown Cotton Fabric	Appliqué
4 Green Polk-a-dot Fabric	Appliqué
5 Off-white Calico Fabric	Appliqué
6 Lt. Brown Cotton Fabric	Appliqué
7 Bright Yellow 4mm Silk	Straight
8 Lt. Green 4mm Silk	Straight (woven)
9 Bright Yellow 4mm Silk	Stem
10 Red 4mm Silk	Straight
11 Lt. Green 4mm Silk	Straight
12 Dk. Brown 4mm Silk	Straight
13 Yellow 4mm Silk	Split
14 Face	Painting on Fabric

Garland of Lights Angel

Enlarge 105 %.

	Fabric/Ribbon/DMC Floss	Method/Stitch
1	Pink Cotton Fabric	Appliqué
2	White Cotton Fabric	Appliqué
3	Brown Cotton Fabric	Appliqué
4	White Gathered Lace	Appliqué
5	Peach Cotton Fabric	Appliqué
6	Lt. Blue Cotton Fabric	Appliqué
7	Peach Cotton Fabric	Appliqué
8	562 floss (1 strand)	Stem
9	562 floss (1 strand)	Straight
10	Blue 4mm Silk	Lazy Daisy
11	Red 4mm Silk	Lazy Daisy
12	White 4mm Silk	Lazy Daisy
13	Lt. Green 4mm Silk	Lazy Daisy
14	Bright Yellow 4mm Silk	Lazy Daisy
15	Dk. Green 4mm Silk	Straight
16	Bright Yellow 4mm Silk	Satin
17	Gold Filament (1 strand)	Straight
18	Yellow 4mm Silk	Chain
19	798 floss (1 strand)	Stem
20	Face	Painting on Fabric

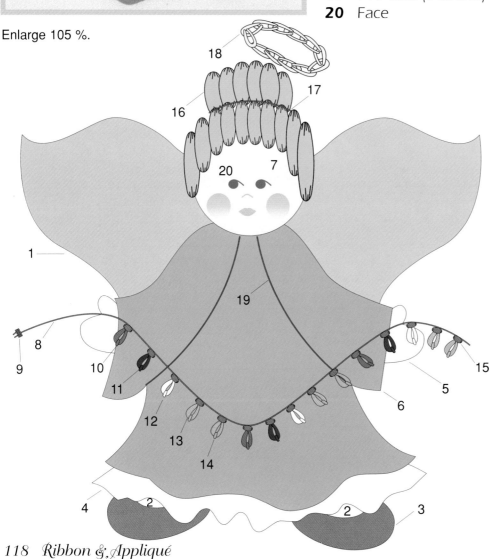

Daffodils

Ribbon/Ribbon Form	Method/Stitch
1 Green 7mm Silk	Straight
2 Green 13mm Silk	One-Twist Ribbon
3 Cream Bud	Dimensional Appliqué (p. 19)
4 Lt. Yellow 7mm Silk	Decorative Lazy Daisy
5 Lt. Yellow 7mm Silk	Straight
6 Small Daffodil Center	Dimensional Appliqué (p. 22)
7 Lt. Yellow 7mm Silk	Lazy Daisy
8 Large Daffodil	Dimensional Appliqué (p. 20)

Additional Design

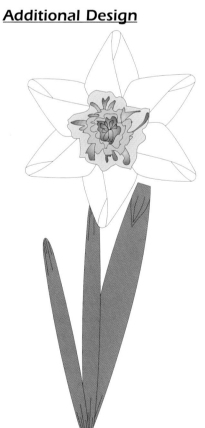

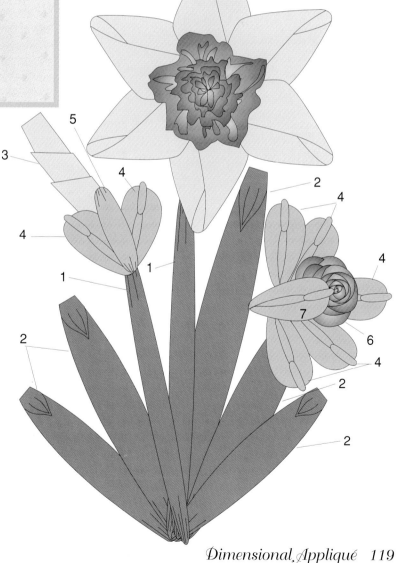

Southern Fan

Ribbon/Ribbon Form	Method/Stitch
1 Fan	Dimensional Appliqué (p. 20)
2 Green 13mm Silk	Bow—Tacking
3 Pink 7mm Silk	Spider Web Rose
4 Yellow 7mm Silk	Spider Web Rose
5 Yellow 7mm Silk	French Knot (2 wraps)

Additional Design

Additional Design

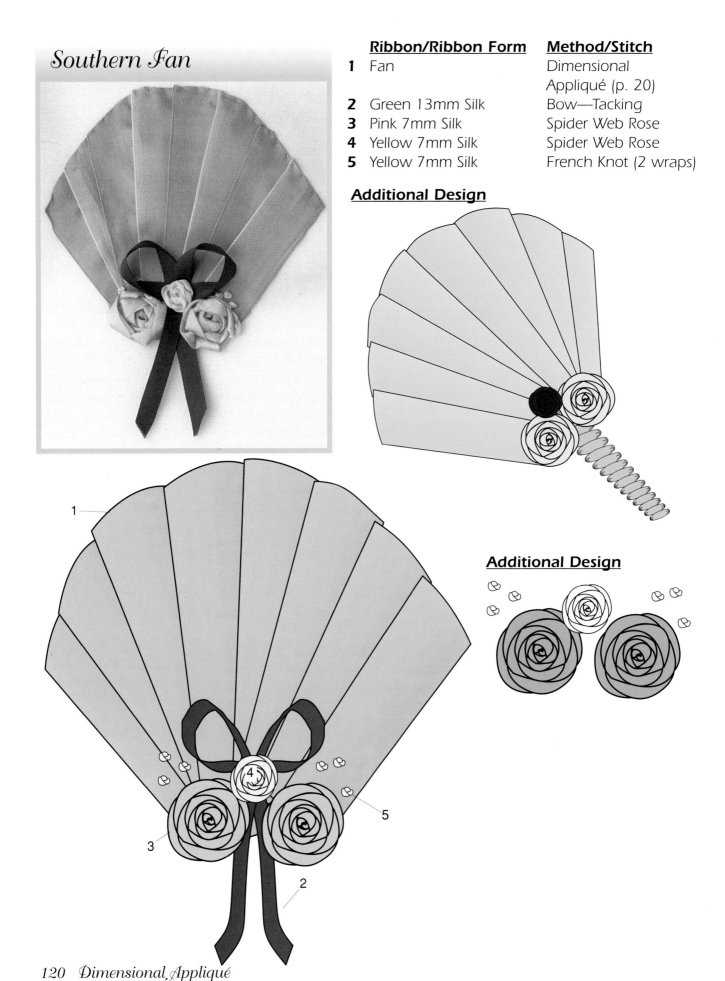

Birdhouse Fence

Ribbon/Ribbon Form/ DMC Floss	Method/Stitch
1 Fence	Dimensional Appliqué (p. 20)
2 Birdhouse	Dimensional Appliqué (p. 19)
3 Brown 4mm Silk	Straight
4 801 floss (6 strands)	Satin
5 895 floss (6 strands)	French Knot (1 wrap)
6 Dk. Green 1" Wired couched with 895 floss (1 strand)	Couched
7 895 floss (2 strands)	Stem
8 Yellow 4mm Silk	Ribbon
9 Dk. Green 4mm Silk	Ribbon

Additional Design

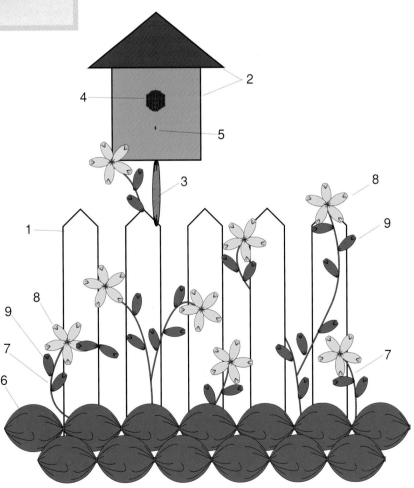

Pansy Nosegay

	Ribbon/Ribbon Form	Method/Stitch
1	Teal 7mm Silk	Whipped Running
2	Aqua 7mm Silk	Whipped Running
3	Teal 7mm Silk	Decorative Lazy Daisy
4	Aqua 7mm Silk	Decorative Lazy Daisy
5	Large Pansy	Dimensional Appliqué (p. 21)
6	Pansy Bud	Dimensional Appliqué (p. 21)
7	Dk. Purple 4mm Silk Purple 4mm Silk	Bow—Tacking

Additional Design

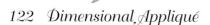

Pink Heart & Rose

Ribbon/Ribbon Form	Method/Stitch
1 Pink Heart	Dimensional Appliqué (p. 21)
2 Pink and Green 1" Variegated tacked with 5mm Pearls	Tacked
3 Pink and Green 1" Variegated	Bow—Tacking
4 Pink Heart Folded Leaf	Dimensional Appliqué (p. 21)
5 Rose	Dimensional Appliqué (p. 22)

Additional Design

Enlarge 135 %.

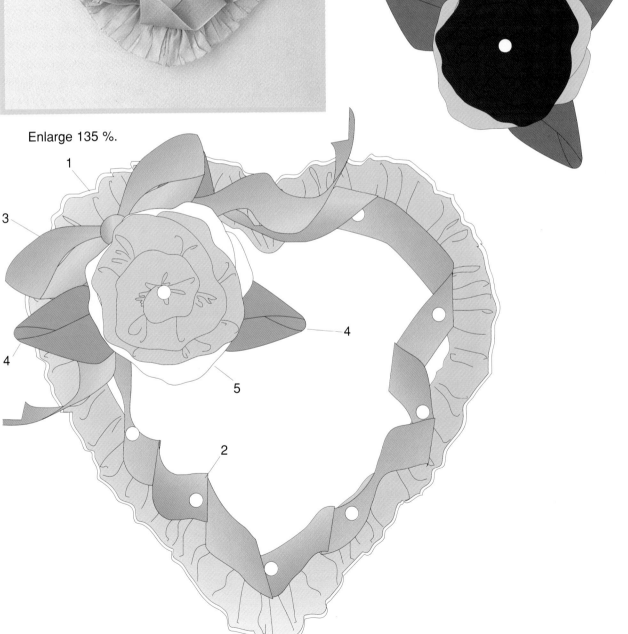

Poppies

	Ribbon/Ribbon Form	Method/Stitch		Ribbon/Ribbon Form	Method/Stitch
1	Gold Wired Braid couched with Gold Fine Braid	Couched	**7**	Large Poppy	Dimensional Appliqué (p. 21)
2	Gold Fine Braid	Couched	**8**	Small Poppy	Dimensional Appliqué (p. 22)
3	Green 13mm Silk	Ribbon	**9**	Green 7mm Silk	Straight
4	Green 7mm Silk	Ribbon	**10**	Green 13mm Silk	Ribbon
5	Red 7mm Silk	Decorative Lazy Daisy	**11**	Black 4mm Silk (double ribbon)	Colonial Knot
6	Green 7mm Silk	Lazy Daisy			

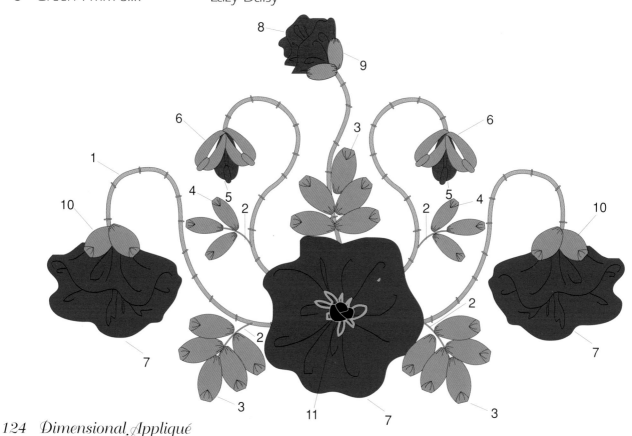

Tea Rose

Ribbon/Ribbon Form/ DMC Floss — Method/Stitch

#	Ribbon/Ribbon Form/DMC Floss	Method/Stitch
1	Folded Leaf	Dimensional Appliqué (p. 20)
2	Small Folded Leaf	Dimensional Appliqué (p. 22)
3	Tea Rosebud	Dimensional Appliqué (p. 22)
4	Lt. Yellow 7mm Silk	Decorative Lazy Daisy
5	Lt. Pink 7mm Silk	Decorative Lazy Daisy
6	Green 7mm Silk	Decorative Lazy Daisy
7	Green 7mm Silk	Ribbon
8	937 floss (6 strands)	Straight
9	Tea Rose	Dimensional Appliqué (p. 23)

Additional Design

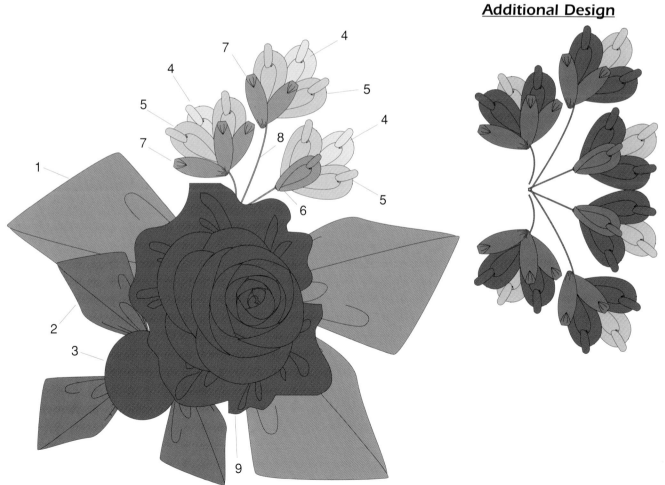

Watering Can

Ribbon/Ribbon Form	Method/Stitch
1 Watering Can	Dimensional Appliqué (p. 23)
2 Silver Heavy Braid	Stem
3 Pink 7mm Organdy	Folded Rose
4 Cream 7mm Silk	Folded Rose
5 Teal 4mm Silk	Lazy Daisy

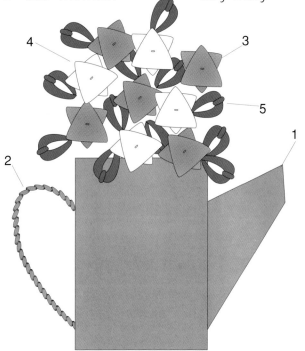

Floral Wagon

Ribbon/Ribbon Form	Method/Stitch
1 Wagon	Dimensional Appliqué (p. 23)
2 Gold 4mm Silk	Stem
3 Gold 4mm Silk	Straight
4 Purple 4mm Silk	Free Form Flower
5 Yellow 7mm Silk	Free Form Flower
6 Pink 7mm Silk	Free Form Flower
7 Dk. Green 7mm Silk	Ribbon

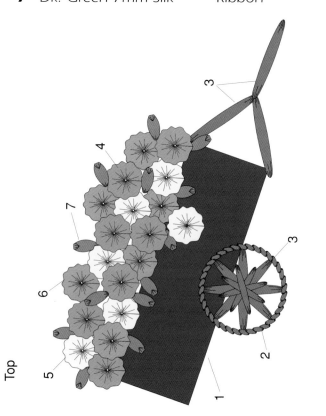

Top

Metric Equivalency Chart

MM-Millimetres   CM-Centimetres

INCHES TO MILLIMETRES AND CENTIMETRES

INCHES	MM	CM	INCHES	CM	INCHES	CM
⅛	3	0.3	9	22.9	30	76.2
¼	6	0.6	10	25.4	31	78.7
½	13	1.3	12	30.5	33	83.8
⅝	16	1.6	13	33.0	34	86.4
¾	19	1.9	14	35.6	35	88.9
⅞	22	2.2	15	38.1	36	91.4
1	25	2.5	16	40.6	37	94.0
1¼	32	3.2	17	43.2	38	96.5
1½	38	3.8	18	45.7	39	99.1
1¾	44	4.4	19	48.3	40	101.6
2	51	5.1	20	50.8	41	104.1
2½	64	6.4	21	53.3	42	106.7
3	76	7.6	22	55.9	43	109.2
3½	89	8.9	23	58.4	44	111.8
4	102	10.2	24	61.0	45	114.3
4½	114	11.4	25	63.5	46	116.8
5	127	12.7	26	66.0	47	119.4
6	152	15.2	27	68.6	48	121.9
7	178	17.8	28	71.1	49	124.5
8	203	20.3	29	73.7	50	127.0

YARDS TO METRES

YARDS	METRES	YARDS	METRES	YARDS	METRES	YARDS	METRES	YARDS	METRES
⅛	0.11	2⅛	1.94	4⅛	3.77	6⅛	5.60	8⅛	7.43
¼	0.23	2¼	2.06	4¼	3.89	6¼	5.72	8¼	7.54
⅜	0.34	2⅜	2.17	4⅜	4.00	6⅜	5.83	8⅜	7.66
½	0.46	2½	2.29	4½	4.11	6½	5.94	8½	7.77
⅝	0.57	2⅝	2.40	4⅝	4.23	6⅝	6.06	8⅝	7.89
¾	0.69	2¾	2.51	4¾	4.34	6¾	6.17	8¾	8.00
⅞	0.80	2⅞	2.63	4⅞	4.46	6⅞	6.29	8⅞	8.12
1	0.91	3	2.74	5	4.57	7	6.40	9	8.23
1⅛	1.03	3⅛	2.86	5⅛	4.69	7⅛	6.52	9⅛	8.34
1¼	1.14	3¼	2.97	5¼	4.80	7¼	6.63	9¼	8.46
1⅜	1.26	3⅜	3.09	5⅜	4.91	7⅜	6.74	9⅜	8.57
1½	1.37	3½	3.20	5½	5.03	7½	6.86	9½	8.69
1⅝	1.49	3⅝	3.31	5⅝	5.14	7⅝	6.97	9⅝	8.80
1¾	1.60	3¾	3.43	5¾	5.26	7¾	7.09	9¾	8.92
1⅞	1.71	3⅞	3.54	5⅞	5.37	7⅞	7.20	9⅞	9.03
2	1.83	4	3.66	6	5.49	8	7.32	10	9.14

Index